Growing Mathematical Ideas in
Kindergarten

Rice)

Growing Mathematical Ideas in Kindergarten

LINDA SCHULMAN DACEY
REBEKA ESTON

Math Solutions Publications
Sausalito, CA

Math Solutions Publications
A division of
Marilyn Burns Education Associates
150 Gate 5 Road, Suite 101
Sausalito, CA 94965
www.mathsolutions.com

Library of Congress Cataloging-in-Publication Data
Schulman, Linda.
    Growing mathematical ideas in kindergarten / Linda Schulman Dacey,
Rebeka Eston.
        p.   cm.
    Includes bibliographical references.
    ISBN 0-941355-22-5 (pbk.)
    1. Mathematics—Study and teaching (Preschool)   I. Eston, Rebeka.
    II. Title.
    QA135.5.S323   1999
    372.7'049—dc21   98-42004
                                                            CIP

Chapter 9, "A Problem Worth Revisiting," was previously published, in a different form, by the National Council of Teachers of Mathematics. Reprinted with permission from *Teaching Children Mathematics*, copyright October, 1998, by the National Council of Teachers of Mathematics.

Figure 8.1, "A Model of the Assessment Cycle," is reprinted by permission of Jean Moon and Linda Schulman: *Finding the Connections: Linking Assessment, Instruction, and Curriculum in Elementary Mathematics* (Heinemann, a division of Reed Elsevier, Inc., Portsmouth, NH, 1995).

Editor: Toby Gordon
Copy editor: Alan Huisman
Production: Alan Huisman
Book design and illustrations: Joni Doherty
Cover design: Leslie Bauman
Cover artwork: Noah Gordon Howland
Composition: Cape Cod Compositors, Inc.

Printed in the United States of America
06   05   04   03   02   01   4   5   6   7   8   9   10

A Message from Marilyn Burns

We at Marilyn Burns Education Associates believe that teaching mathematics well calls for continually reflecting on and improving one's instructional practice. Our Math Solutions Publications include a wide range of choices, from books in our new Teaching Arithmetic series—which address beginning number concepts, place value, addition, subtraction, multiplication, division, fractions, decimals, and percents—to resources that help link math with writing and literature; from books that help teachers more deeply understand the mathematics behind the math they teach to children's books that help students develop an appreciation for math while learning basic concepts.

Along with our large collection of teacher resource books, we have a more general collection of books, videotapes, and audiotapes that can help teachers and parents bridge the gap between home and school. All of our materials are available at education stores, from distributors, and through major teacher catalogs.

In addition, Math Solutions Inservice offers five-day courses and one-day workshops throughout the country. We also work in partnership with school districts to help implement and sustain long-term improvement in mathematics instruction in all classrooms.

To find a complete listing of our publications and workshops, please visit our Web site at *www.mathsolutions.com*. Or contact us by calling (800) 868-9092 or sending an e-mail to *info@math-solutions.com*. We're eager for your feedback and interested in learning about your particular needs. We look forward to hearing from you.

A DIVISION OF MARILYN BURNS EDUCATION ASSOCIATES

To our grandchildren,

Brianna,

Liam,

Madelyn,

& Savanna.

We wish them kindergarten classrooms
in which mathematical ideas flourish.

Contents

Foreword

Marilyn Burns

The first time I taught a math lesson in a kindergarten class, I had been a teacher for six years and my entire experience had been teaching mathematics to eighth graders. A kindergarten teacher in my district, a friend of mine, told me she found teaching mathematics to eighth graders a terrifying thought. She wasn't sure which seemed more frightening, the math, dealing with adolescents, or the teaching load of 150 students in five different classes.

I finally confessed my own fears about teaching kindergarten. What was the math at that level? What were children that age capable of understanding? What were they able to do? And what did a teacher do with the same class for all those hours? However, since I was at the time beginning to present math workshops to teachers, I thought that experience with kindergartners would be useful. I volunteered to teach a lesson to her class.

I decided to collect information from the children, organize the information into a graph, and then discuss with the class what the graph showed. I would focus on the number of syllables in the children's first names. "How many claps are there for your first name?" I would ask. I'd use my own name as a model. *"Ma - ri - lyn* has three claps," I'd say, clapping once for each syllable.

Then I'd write my name in the "3" column on chart paper that I had ruled into four columns labeled "1," "2," "3," and "4."

The day for the lesson came. I remember it well. The children gathered on the rug. I demonstrated why *Marilyn* has three claps and then said, "Now, you'll each figure out the number of claps in your own name." Before I could give more directions, most of the children started clapping their hands. Some seemed to be saying their name as well, but most just seemed to be clapping. Enthusiastically. One boy was clapping loudly, close to his neighbor's ear. She winced, then finally got annoyed and shouted, "Stop, Tommy!"

My friend whose class it was helped me restore order. She told the children they would have to take turns and clap one at a time. I asked a girl near the front to stand up. Her name was Ann, she told me. "Okay—Ann" I said, repeating her name and clapping once. Somehow, a name with only one clap didn't sound very interesting to me. Or to the children. I wrote "Ann" on the chart in the "1" column.

"Why do you think I wrote Ann's name in this column?" I asked. There was silence. Some children shrugged. "What's a collin?" one boy asked. "It's a one," a girl stated in a tone that indicated she thought the reason was obvious. Other children began to chant, "It's a one. It's a one." Some began to clap again.

My friend again quieted her students. "Why did I write 'Marilyn' under the three?" I continued. The responses varied. "You're bigger." "Three's my favorite number." "I like four better." "It had three claps." "Where's the three?" "Can I do my name?"

Ann was still standing, looking confused. I asked her to sit down and called on the loud clapper from before.

"I'm Tom," he said.

"No, you're not," another boy said. "You're Tommy."

"Well, my real name is Thomas."

"Sometimes my dad calls me Annie," Ann chimed in.

"I have two names, my first name and a middle name," another girl said.

"I have a middle name too."

"Me too."

This time I was ready. I called the class to attention myself. I was used to teaching volatile eighth graders and could manage classes well. But somehow this was different.

"What name would you like to use for our graph?" I asked Tom.

"Tom," he said.

"Okay," I responded, "let's clap together." Again, one syllable, one clap. The children (and I) were wondering why this activity was such a good idea.

"Let's have Elizabeth go next," my friend said. I shot her a heartfelt look of gratitude. Elizabeth came up, and she and I clapped four times for her name—*E - liz - a - beth*. Then the rest of the children said *Elizabeth* and clapped. Now we were making progress.

"Raise your hand if you know where I should write 'Elizabeth' on our graph," I said. Most children shot up a hand. The rest raised theirs as soon as they noticed the other children had.

I pointed to the first column, labeled "1," in which I had written "Ann" and "Tom." "Who thinks that I should write 'Elizabeth' in this column?" Some hands went down. Some stayed up. I pointed to the column labeled "2" and repeated the question. Different hands went up; others went down; some that had been raised in response to my first question stayed raised. "And here?" I asked, pointing to the third column. Again, some hands stayed up, others went up, others went down. I pointed to the fourth column. "And here?" Hands stayed up, went down, went up. I forged ahead. "I'm going to write 'Elizabeth' under the four because *Elizabeth* has four claps."

You get the gist. The lesson was nuts, far from my finest hour. By the end I was exhausted. I learned from the experience, but it didn't do much to build my confidence.

I taught that lesson more than twenty-five years ago. Since then I've visited other kindergarten classes and taught more lessons. My respect has grown for the challenge of working with young children and helping give them a sound base of mathematics on which they will build throughout their schooling.

When I read the manuscript of Linda and Becky's book, I was thrilled. The educational and mathematics rationales are clear; the classroom descriptions breathe life into sound theoretical underpinnings; the suggestions offered are sensible, practical, and supportive. *If only I had been able to read this book before I ventured into a kindergarten class,* I thought, *I would have had a context for thinking about young children and how they learn mathematics.* And even with the experience I've accumulated from my years of teaching, the book is motivating, confirming my beliefs about teaching mathematics, and wonderfully useful for applying my beliefs to teaching young children. I'm pleased Linda and Becky have written it, and I'm pleased to have published it. This book can help anyone interested in helping young children make sense of mathematics. Read it!

Preface

Rebeka Eston

I am humbled by the book you are about to read. Never in my wildest dreams did I imagine it would exist. And it wouldn't if not for the foresight, persistence, and unwavering dedication of Linda Schulman Dacey.

One never truly knows when the seeds of ideas are first planted. I have known and respected Linda for almost two decades. When we met, I was an undergraduate student at Lesley College, rediscovering the joy of learning mathematics (something I lost in junior high). Several years ago we reconnected at a Lesley College summer institute focusing on alternative assessment. More recently, we had an opportunity to share ideas while working in a study group she led at my school. During this time, she visited my kindergarten classroom and suggested writing an article about our work. From this article, which was published in *Teaching Children Mathematics,* came the idea for this book. At the time I was in no way ready to embark on so new and so long a journey, but Linda convinced me that there was a story to be shared, and so we began.

Linda breathed life into this project from the beginning. She began to piece this story together through her careful observations and our countless conversations. It is her knowledge, her passion for teaching and learning mathematics, and her willingness to listen without judgment that have given form to this book. She believed in this project, in my students, and in me. What more can a coauthor and friend ask for? I am deeply grateful.

This book is about kindergarten and the wonderful children who work and play there. It is about teaching and learning mathematics. And, yes, it is about me and my journey as a kindergarten teacher. Linda takes all of these facets and weaves them together to tell a story of which I am very proud, a story about the role mathematics can play in the lives of five- and six-year-olds.

Kindergarten is a special beginning, a demarcation. It is a time of childhood wonder and delight, of fears and adventures. It can be the start of a lifelong exploration of mathematical ideas, or it can lay the first stones in the wall between real math and school math that is so often built when children "learn" rather than "live" mathematics.

This wall can be avoided in active kindergarten classrooms where instruction is based on meaningful mathematical inquiry. In such classrooms, students explore mathematics in contexts that make sense to them, develop their own mathematical procedures and representations, and are involved in conversations that support the generation of mathematical ideas. *Kindergarten* is a German word meaning children's garden, and I like to think this approach to teaching and learning is the growing of mathematical ideas.

I have taught for eighteen years, fourteen of them in kindergarten classrooms. I teach kindergarten because I want to help children develop a love of learning from the beginning. If my classroom is a garden in which children can grow and flourish, it is because of the innumerable tangible and intangible contributions made by my family, friends, colleagues, teachers, and mentors. Fertile ground does not come easy. It is a cumulative effect. There are more people for me to thank than I can ever begin to say. I can only hope that they realize how truly grateful I am.

So often, teaching is considered an isolating profession. This has not been my experience. I share my classroom daily with wonderful children. I teach alongside some of the best professionals in the field. I am fortunate enough to work in a town whose citizens believe so strongly in quality education that they are willing to support it at every turn. As a direct result, I believe I have had opportunities for professional growth and success not available to many teachers.

When Linda first suggested writing about my classroom, I was just completing five years of intense professional development as a member of two NSF-funded projects: Talking Mathematics and Teaching to the Big Ideas. Through these projects I established connections with TERC and went on to work on the Investigations curriculum for kindergarten. I will always be grateful to Rebecca Corwin, Deborah Schifter, Susan Jo Russell, Virginia Bastable, Sophia Cohen, and Karen Economopoulos, who, in their various roles on these projects, modeled what it means to be a teacher—a professional—and who have encouraged me to believe in what I think.

The pages of this book are alive with the voices of my students. Even though their names have been changed, they speak for themselves. What they and all the children who have graced my classroom before them have taught me cannot be bought or sold. They have given me countless treasures. I am truly blessed and very grateful.

Also in these pages are names of colleagues who have taught me equally well: Carolyn Casey, Marie Crispen, Bobbi Fisher, Joanne McManus, Margy Roy, and Geneva Smithlin. They represent many more educators (past and present) in the Lincoln Public Schools who, together with peers on professional development projects, have touched my life as only teachers can. It has made a significant difference. Thank you!

Acknowledgments

First, thank you to the children in Becky's classroom, whose voices resonate throughout this book. Their imagination and curiosity have been a delight. Similarly, we thank Becky's colleagues and her principal, Joanne McManus, for their continuous and unstinting support throughout this project and Becky's career at the Lincoln Public Schools.

A heartfelt acknowledgment to Karen Economopoulos, who reviewed every chapter and guided our work so well, and to aspiring teacher Julienne Webster, for her immeasurable contributions. And thanks to Brianna Fay, Amy Gartland, and Leslie Daly for their help preparing the manuscript.

We thank our editor, Toby Gordon, for her endless guidance and support, and both Toby and Marilyn Burns for their profound insight. Thank you, too, to Alan Huisman and to the many other talented people we have encountered at Math Solutions.

Finally, we want to acknowledge the two people who sustain us most. By coincidence, they are both named John. We thank them for their continuous love, support, assurance, patience, encouragement, and friendship, and for always being there.

1

A Vision for Growing Mathematical Ideas in Kindergarten

"**M**ama," Nicole whispered anxiously as she held her mother's hand in the aisle of the local grocery store, "that's my teacher." It was clear from her wide-eyed look that Nicole was not sure what to make of seeing her teacher in this setting. Everything about Nicole's body language said, What are you doing here? For Becky, Nicole's kindergarten teacher, this was a familiar experience. There is often a similar reaction whenever one of her students sees her outside school for the first time.

If students do not have occasion to see their teachers outside the school environment, the teachers' image is limited to the one they present within the school walls. The same can be said of students' sense of mathematics. Many children never experience mathematics instruction organized to build mathematical ideas and to integrate those ideas into the real world. Their image of mathematics and their ability to do mathematics, then, is limited to the performance of isolated skills in the classroom.

Becky's first reaction to seeing her students outside school is predictable, too. She almost always thinks, When did you get so small? How is it possible that the children she expects to make sense of the complexities of mathematics look so young and dependent? What mathematical ideas can she expect such small children to grasp?

Young children have preliminary mathematical ideas about counting, comparative and positional relationships, money, shapes, and patterns long before they enter the kindergarten classroom. They have formed ideas—not isolated skills—that are rooted firmly in real-world contexts. These ideas have developed from children's natural curiosity about the world around them. Once they come to school, however, many of them develop a sense of school math, a collection of fragmented rote skills disconnected from the real world.

Mathematics in the Kindergarten Classroom

Ideally, Becky's classroom builds on children's natural curiosity and carefully avoids the false dichotomy between school math and real math. Questions, often posed by the children, tap this curiosity and are woven into the curriculum. By being able to ask questions that receive attention (*How many days to my birthday? Is my shadow always shorter than me?*), children gain respect for their role in the learning process. By exploring these questions, children make connections: between the calendar and important dates, between the time of day and the length of a shadow. These connections help them make sense of the world.

When children are "sense making" through their activities and interactions, they gain self-confidence. This greater sense of confidence helps them take greater risks in their explorations, and they become even more curious. New questions—*Does someone else in class have a birthday before mine? Does the length of my shadow change in the winter?*—are posed. (See Figure 1.1.)

Becky's goal is to create a classroom that encourages children's curiosity, prompts them to explore that curiosity, leads them to make connections, and builds their confidence. To tap their mathematical curiosity, she molds a curriculum that motivates children to engage in mathematical investigations that are relevant to them. She selects open-ended tasks that allow all children to take part in the exploration regardless of their develop-

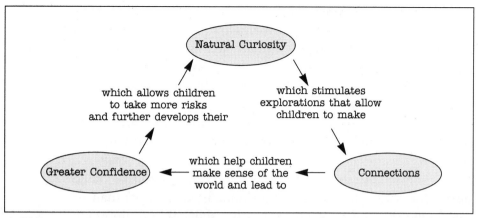

FIGURE 1.1   The causal, self-perpetuating loop between curiosity, connections, and confidence

mental level or learning style. Since Becky does not define how they are to explore the tasks, the children are naturally drawn to developmentally appropriate pathways. They choose approaches that best fit their own level of thinking.

As Becky's students strive to understand their world through mathematical explorations, they talk about the connections they are making. By manipulating objects and talking about their experiences, they construct knowledge. Their classroom community respects ideas and inquiry. The communication and representation of their techniques and findings are a necessary part of the experience and thus are valued. Over time and through reflection, the children refine their ideas and pose new questions.

Becky has a passion for studying the thinking of children. As she spends more time *listening to* children and less time *speaking at* them, she gains a greater appreciation for the complexity and diversity of the learning process. Over time, this understanding has helped her better design, choose, and sequence appropriate tasks. Her sense of the learning path is continually revised based on student feedback.

Studying children's thinking has given Becky a greater appreciation for mathematics. Too often the kindergarten mathematics program is limited to developing rote skills associated with counting and with recognizing shapes. Unfortunately, this limited perspective of mathematics is often reinforced at home as parents begin to prepare their children for "school math": many children learn early on that mathematics is only counting and naming shapes. While parents similarly reinforce recognizing letters and associating those letters with their corresponding sounds, this attention to isolated, rote skills is balanced by the holistic joy of reading a story. Although holistic mathematical activities also occur in the home—playing with blocks and doing puzzles, for example—they are rarely identified as mathematical activities.

It is essential, then, that mathematics instruction be based on a broader view, be focused on meaningful ideas rather than on rote skills. This does not mean that the skills are unimportant; however, they need to be learned within the context of mathematical ideas. Too many people think that teaching skills and concepts is either-or. This is not the case. Mathematical ideas help children *understand* and *connect* the skills they develop. When that happens, children are more likely to remember the skills and apply them when they are needed.

A Week in the Life

How does a classroom that is focused on building ideas work? The best way to get a sense of this is to eavesdrop on a week of mathematics in Becky's classroom. It is late September; the topic is patterns; the activities are adapted from Investigations in Number, Data and Space, *Pattern Trains and Hopscotch Paths* (Eston and Economopoulos 1998).

Since the beginning of the year, the students have played a game, Copy Cat, in which they mimic a sequence of two physical motions. For example, as the children gather in the meeting area, Becky might slap her knees, clap her hands, slap her knees, clap her hands, repeatedly, until all the children have joined her. However, there has been no discussion about what a pattern is or how the children know what to do next when they explore the rhythmic actions. It is time to dig deeper.

Becoming familiar with patterns is important groundwork for mathematical thinking and for later work with numbers. Traditional work with patterns focuses on children's abilities to copy, extend, create, and record patterns. Since *Mathematics Their Way*

(Baratta-Lorton 1976) was published, kindergarten teachers have devoted considerable attention to children's ability to develop these important skills. Becky has used these activities for many years, and they have withstood the test of time. She now believes, however, that the skills developed through these tasks become more powerful when tied to essential ideas about patterns and mathematics.

Becky wants her students to understand the essence of what a pattern is and why it is helpful to recognize patterns. She wants their individual skills to be grounded in the idea that patterns can be extended and generalized. She wants her students to know that they can make predictions based on information available to them, that they can find patterns all around them, and that patterns themselves can be categorized and recorded.

Monday

The children are gathered in a circle in the meeting area. Becky has a bucket of Unifix cubes with her, along with two preassembled trains of eight cubes each. The first train has eight cubes of random colors. The second train is an alternating red, white, red, white (A–B) pattern. Becky holds up the random train.

BECKY: WHAT DO YOU NOTICE ABOUT THIS TRAIN?

KIMI: There's only one of each color.

BEN: Every cube is snapped together.

ALLISON: It has eight pieces.

BECKY: [*Holding up the train with the alternating pattern*] WHAT DO YOU NOTICE ABOUT THIS TRAIN?

ANA: It's a pattern.

JAMAL: It has two colors.

SAMMY: It has four reds.

HALEY: And four white.

ALLISON: It's not like the other one.

JAMAL: They both have eight.

BECKY: WHAT'S DIFFERENT ABOUT THESE TWO TRAINS?

SETH: Not all the same colors.

BECKY: ANA SAID THAT THIS ONE [*holding up the train with the alternating pattern*] IS A PATTERN. IS THIS ONE [*holding up the train with random colors*] A PATTERN? [*There is a chorus of nos.*] WHAT MAKES THIS ONE [*again holding up the train with the alternating pattern*] A PATTERN?

ANA: It has white, red, white, red. It's a pattern.

BECKY: WHAT'S A PATTERN?

TREVOR: It's when there is one color, then another color, then the other color, then the other color.

BECKY: CAN THERE BE YELLOW IN THIS PATTERN?

SETH: No, because it's red, white, red, white.

ALLISON: You can put yellow, blue, yellow, blue.

BECKY: [*Adding these cubes to the train*] WHAT DO YOU THINK?

MEGAN: It's two patterns.

MARIO: There's the red, white, and then the yellow, blue.

Some teachers would not have added the yellow and blue cubes to the train. Instead, they might have said something like, Yes, yellow, blue, yellow, blue, is like red, white, red, white. Becky prefers to follow the children's lead and let them pose their own questions and draw their own conclusions. It is the children who need to wrestle with how these two patterns are the same and how they are different.

Following this discussion, Becky separates the children into groups so that they can begin making patterns with materials. In assigning the groups, she makes sure that each one includes both girls and boys. Over the course of the year other criteria may emerge. She may identify a pair of children who work particularly well together and frequently place them in the same group. Similarly, there may be children she often separates because she believes they distract each other or are too dependent on each other. Becky's groups are most often heterogeneous, although occasionally she selects a group of children with similar needs in order to work with them directly.

The children are assigned to work areas with teddy bear counters or Unifix cubes. (Becky has borrowed materials from the teacher next door in order to have enough for groups to work with the same materials.) As the children work, Becky visits with groups of children individually, asking them to describe their patterns or explain their thinking. She makes notes about their conversations and products as she moves from group to group. She records the language the children use to describe their work: "It repeats." "It's a pattern." "It goes this, then that." She notes who makes a pattern and the type of pattern she or he makes. (Chapter 8 discusses in depth the ways in which Becky documents learning.)

Most of the children build similar alternating patterns. The work of some children stands out. All of Mario's patterns use reds and whites, and the first pattern he makes has exactly eight cubes. Becky makes a note to herself to check Mario's choice of colors tomorrow. She wants to see whether he will again be restricted by her examples. Ezra and Allison each make a pattern with three alternating colors (A–B–C). Nicole builds a train of blue, black, blue, white, black, red, blue.

Becky asks Nicole to describe her pattern, wanting to see whether her question will cause Nicole to rethink her work. Nicole points to each cube and names the color. Becky does not probe further, because she does not want to make Nicole self-conscious about her work. An initial question often makes a child feel that his or her work is respected. Too many questions can cause a loss of confidence. Becky has learned to be patient and not pass judgment on children's early work. She wants the children to learn how to judge their own work.

When the activity ends, Becky asks four of the children if she can save their trains for later discussion. She will use these patterns the next day.

Tuesday
The class gathers in a circle in the meeting area.

BECKY: KIMI, RORY, BEN, ALLISON, HERE ARE YOUR TRAINS. CAN YOU TELL US ABOUT THEM?

KIMI: I made mine green, blue, green, blue, green, blue.

RORY: Mine's red, blue, red, blue.

BEN: I did brown, yellow, brown, yellow.

ALLISON: Mine's red, blue, green, red, blue, green.

BECKY: HOW ARE THESE TRAINS ALIKE?

MEI: They all use colors and cubes.

KAITLIN: They're patterns.

BECKY: HOW ARE THEY DIFFERENT?

SAMMY: Allison used three colors.

MEI:	The others are two.
BECKY:	IS ALLISON'S STILL A PATTERN?
MARIO:	I think so.
KIMI:	It goes red, blue, green, red, blue, green.

The children seem to recognize that the A–B pattern is different from an A–B–C pattern. They have begun to categorize their products.

Following this discussion, the children work in the same groups as yesterday. The children will remain in the same group throughout the week, so that Becky can easily keep track of the progress they make and the materials they use. Keeping the groups the same also allows them to develop their own language to describe their patterns and helps them feel safe.

Today there are four types of materials available: Unifix cubes, teddy bear counters, pattern blocks, and color tiles. Becky makes sure that the groups have time to make patterns at two work areas, one with a material available yesterday, and one with a new material. Repeating similar activities helps children feel confident in their work. Introducing different materials stimulates their thinking and broadens their notion of patterns.

In general, the children use the materials in different ways. Teddy bear patterns tend to be built in circles or in pairs, because children personify these figures; the basic repeating units are often referred to as teams, partners, or families. Unifix cubes lend themselves to "trains"—patterns in a line—because they snap together in only one way. The color tiles do not restrict children in this manner. Almost half the children using color tiles make patterns in the shape of an L. For example, here is Trevor's:

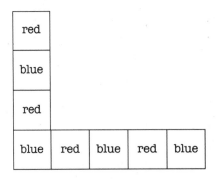

Using pattern blocks presents noteworthy challenges, because they provide the opportunity for children to see patterns that alternate in shape as well as color. Given the nature of these materials students may also create constructions that are pictures or designs rather than patterns. Becky recognizes the natural tendency of children to use pattern blocks this way and has thought about not including these materials in early pattern investigations. However, she has decided working with pattern blocks helps children clarify their notion of what makes a pattern. They need to decide whether or not the figures they generate are patterns or not.

Today, Kaitlin makes the symmetric design shown in Figure 1.2. Her construction does not show a pattern. Becky wants to know more about Kaitlin's thinking.

FIGURE 1.2 Kaitlin's symmetric construction

BECKY: ARE YOU MAKING A PATTERN, KAITLIN?

KAITLIN: I'm just making something. It's sort of a pattern.

BECKY: WHAT DO YOU MEAN?

KAITLIN: I'm not sure.

BECKY: [*Probing deeper*] CAN YOU MAKE SOMETHING THAT YOU'RE
           SURE IS A PATTERN?

KAITLIN: I don't know, but I like this one.

Becky decides not to pursue the matter further. Kaitlin has begun to sense a difference between patterns and designs; that is enough for now. Becky used to "teach" children what a design was and what a pattern was as a way to introduce the use of pattern blocks. Now she doesn't introduce this topic until the children have begun to differentiate the two on their own. This way, she helps the children build the idea themselves, with their own language and examples. Further, she does not limit them from creating designs that can then be repeated to make patterns. In a few weeks there will be a large-group discussion about patterns and designs, and the children will build on their own ideas. Eventually they will come to understand that a pattern can be extended and generalized.

As Becky reviews the notes she has taken as the children worked, she decides that they are progressing rather quickly. Almost one fourth of them have now built a pattern with more than two colors. She decides to introduce them to patterns other than A–B patterns more formally.

Wednesday

Because of the bus schedules at Becky's school, children enter the classroom over a ten-minute period. Becky often uses "question cards" to take advantage of their staggered arrival. Children respond individually to a written question that sets the stage for the day's focus. (Becky knows the children cannot read the words independently, but exposing children to written text is an important goal of her literacy program.)

When the children arrive today, there is the beginning of a Unifix train and a question card on the table as they enter the room:

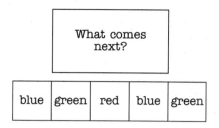

| What comes next? | | | | |
| blue | green | red | blue | green |

Since it is late September, the children have encountered question cards several times before, but this is the first one related to patterns.

Rory is the first child who enters, and Becky reads him the question. There is a bucket of Unifix cubes on the table, and Rory adds the cube that he thinks comes next. Rory tells Ana, the next child to enter, what is written on the card, and she adds a cube. Becky stays near the table but lets the children negotiate the activity themselves as much as possible. After all the children have arrived, added a cube, and settled in, Becky leads the morning meeting and then it's time for gym. As Becky walks the children to meet their gym teacher, she says, "When you come back we'll talk about the pattern you made this morning when you came into the room."

When Becky returns to the classroom and looks at the train, she faces a dilemma: the children have created a train with no apparent pattern. She is not sure what has gone wrong. Has she misjudged their understanding of pattern? Should her initial model have included two complete repetitions of the core unit? As is so often the case for teachers, there is no time for her to reflect further on causation. She has to decide what to do. She wants to use the children's work to motivate the discussion when they return but believes that focusing on this train will only confuse their thinking. Yet she does not want to dismantle the children's work as such an action might suggest that it is not valued.

In the end, Becky focuses on what action will best develop children's understanding of patterns. It is clear to her that the train the children have created is not going to foster the growth of ideas. While she is not looking for a "perfect" piece of work, she thinks the series of blocks is too random and will not motivate a meaningful discussion. She decides to set up a new pattern for the children to complete when they return from gym.

She's not sure what caused the difficulty in the first pattern, so she decides to use only two colors (different ones from those she used in her original pattern that morning) and provides two complete cycles of the repeating pattern: orange, orange, brown, orange, orange, brown. (She does want the children's notion of pattern to deepen, so she does not go back to an A–B pattern.)

As the children reenter the classroom, they are each asked to add a cube to the new train. Most children follow the implied A–A–B pattern successfully, although two do not. The children settle in a circle and Becky shows them the new train.

ALLISON: What happened to our other pattern?

BECKY: [*Thinking that the class never lets her get away with anything*] I GOT CONFUSED WHEN I LOOKED AT THE FIRST TRAIN, SO I DECIDED TO TRY A DIFFERENT ONE.

ALLISON: I'm glad. That other one was hard.

BECKY: WHAT MADE THE OTHER ONE HARD?

TREVOR: It had three kinds.

BECKY: WAS THIS ONE EASIER? [*There is a chorus of yeses.*] WHAT MADE IT EASIER?

SAMMY: It just has two colors.

JAMAL: There's something wrong with this pattern.

EZRA: I was going to say that, too.

BECKY: HOW DO YOU KNOW THERE IS SOMETHING WRONG WITH THE PATTERN?

JAMAL: I can see it.

BECKY: DOES ANYONE ELSE SEE IT TOO? [*Many nod their head.*] CAN WE FIX THIS?

TANYA: We could put in another orange one here. [*She points to the section of the train shown below.*]

orange	orange	brown	orange	orange	brown	orange	brown	orange	orange	brown

BECKY: DO YOU THINK THAT WOULD WORK? [*There is another chorus of yeses, and Tanya adds the orange block.*] IS THERE ANYTHING ELSE THAT NEEDS TO BE FIXED?

KAITLIN: The two browns. [*She points to the section of the train shown below.*]

orange	orange	brown	orange	orange	brown	brown	orange	orange	brown	

↑

BECKY: WHAT CAN WE DO ABOUT THIS?

KAITLIN: [*Starts to take the train apart at the two browns, but stops, apparently unsure of what to do next; then, starting at the beginning of the train, she points to each cube and whispers the color of the block until she comes to the two browns and removes one of the browns with confidence*] It works!

BECKY: YOU KNOW HOW WE DO OUR READING TOGETHER WHEN I POINT TO THE WORDS? WE CAN SAY THE COLORS AS I POINT TO THE CUBES.

EVERYONE: Orange, orange, brown, orange, orange, brown . . .

BECKY: NOW I HAVE A QUESTION FOR YOU TO THINK ABOUT. HOW DO YOU KNOW WHAT COMES NEXT?

TREVOR: 'Cause there's an orange, orange, brown, and then you do it all over again.

HALEY: By looking at it.

BECKY: WHAT DO YOU LOOK AT?

HALEY: I look at the pattern.

BECKY: WHAT PART OF THIS IS THE PATTERN?

KAITLIN: The colors. I think in my head about what comes next.

BECKY: WHEN YOU WORK IN YOUR GROUPS TODAY MAKING PATTERNS, THINK ABOUT HOW YOU KNOW WHAT COMES NEXT.

Becky breathes a sigh of relief. The activity hasn't followed the straightest path, but it has achieved what she intended. The children have begun to recognize that a repeating pattern is built from a core unit that must remain the same in each repetition. They have all been exposed to a pattern other than the basic A–B pattern. She sends the children off to work in groups, eager to see the patterns they will build.

The children again use the four materials to make patterns. Children using the color tiles begin making rectangular shapes as well as Ls. Allison piles up tiles in an A–A–B pattern, calling it her "pattern sandwich." The trains made of Unifix cubes are getting much longer. There are several A–B–C patterns at the teddy bear table. Becky moves from group to group, recording observations and asking, "How did you know what to put next?" Children point and say the color or shape of each item in their patterns.

Thursday

The groups are assigned so that the children are working with a material they did not use yesterday. The children build patterns steadily for about ten minutes before Becky announces that in a couple of minutes she wants them to look at other children's work. This "debriefing" allows the children to reflect on their work and further define their understanding of what a pattern is. All the children join Becky at the work station with Unifix cubes.

BECKY: LISA, TELL US ABOUT YOUR WORK.

LISA: It goes red, red, blue, red, red, blue, red, red, blue, and it keeps going on forever.

BECKY: HOW DO YOU KNOW IT GOES ON FOREVER?

LISA: 'Cause you can never stop a pattern.

After moving from station to station, with all the children being given an opportunity to share their patterns, the class returns to the meeting area. Becky begins a game of Copy Cat. This is the first time the children have played the game since they have explored and discussed patterns. After they have followed the alternating pattern for several rounds, Becky starts a discussion.

BECKY: WHAT DID WE JUST DO?

TREVOR: We made a pattern with our hands.

BECKY:	ARE THERE OTHER WAYS WE COULD MAKE PATTERNS?
MEI:	I can make a pattern with my dog.
BECKY:	HOW DO YOU DO THAT, MEI?
MEI:	I throw a ball and my dog brings it back. I throw a ball and my dog brings it back.
TREVOR:	I have a pattern on my shirt! It goes yellow, green, white, yellow, green, white.
KIMI:	I have a pattern on my shirt.
RORY:	Look, I have a pattern on my shirt too!
BECKY:	WELL, THIS IS AMAZING. I BET YOU COULD FIND PATTERNS IN MANY PLACES. NOW, BEFORE WE BEGIN OUR STORY, I WANT TO COMPLIMENT YOU ON HOW YOU WORKED TODAY. YOU SHARED THE MATERIALS WELL. YOU WORKED HARD. YOU STAYED IN YOUR GROUPS AND YOU FOLLOWED DIRECTIONS. DOES ANYONE ELSE HAVE A COMPLIMENT TO GIVE?
MEI:	Rory shared his red bears with me.
BEN:	Ezra helped me fix my pattern.

As Becky reflects on the children's progress, she thinks about the ideas she wants them to understand about patterns. All the children can recognize and produce an A–B pattern and are developing an understanding that patterns can help them predict what comes next. They have begun to recognize that patterns can be found everywhere. In fact, later in the day, Mei chooses to work in the art center and draws a pattern with flowers (see Figure 1.3). Becky thinks it's time to introduce a new pattern activity, one that will help the children focus on using the core unit of a pattern (the basic sequence that is then repeated) to predict what comes next.

FIGURE 1.3 Mei's flower pattern

Friday

On the chalkboard near the meeting area, Becky has hung a pocket chart made up of ten rows of ten clear plastic pockets. She has prearranged a pattern of color squares in three of the rows. Only the beginning colors of each pattern can be seen; the rest are hidden behind cards with question marks on them. (See Figure 1.4.) Becky has chosen an A–B pattern for the first row because she wants to begin with the type of pattern that is most familiar to the children. An A–B–B pattern is used in the second row, in order to challenge children's expectations. The A–B–C pattern in the third row will further expand children's thinking.

This activity helps the children focus on how a pattern can be used to make predictions, because a variety of correct options for continuing a pattern are possible. For example, the orange, yellow, in the second row could lead to an A–B, A–B–B, A–B–C, or A–B–A pattern. Students do not necessarily consider these alternatives when they merely add cubes onto a train. Using a pattern chart like this gives them a chance to verify their thinking. Through repeated experiences with this activity, the children begin to consider a greater variety of options for what *could* come next. Further, since the children want to predict what *does* come next, this activity emphasizes how important it is for them to think about what they know and when they know it. It initiates them into a mathematical journey that will continue in later years, when the question *How do you know?* becomes *Can you prove it?*

The children gather at the meeting area and immediately notice the new pocket chart.

TREVOR: What's that?

BECKY: WHAT DO YOU SEE?

TREVOR: You're trying to make a pattern.

BECKY: HOW DO YOU KNOW?

ALLISON: I see yellow, brown, yellow, brown.

BECKY: [*Pointing to the first question mark after the four color squares*] HOW MANY PEOPLE THINK THERE WILL BE A YELLOW HERE? [*Many hands raise.*] HOW DO YOU KNOW WHEN YOU CAN'T SEE IT?

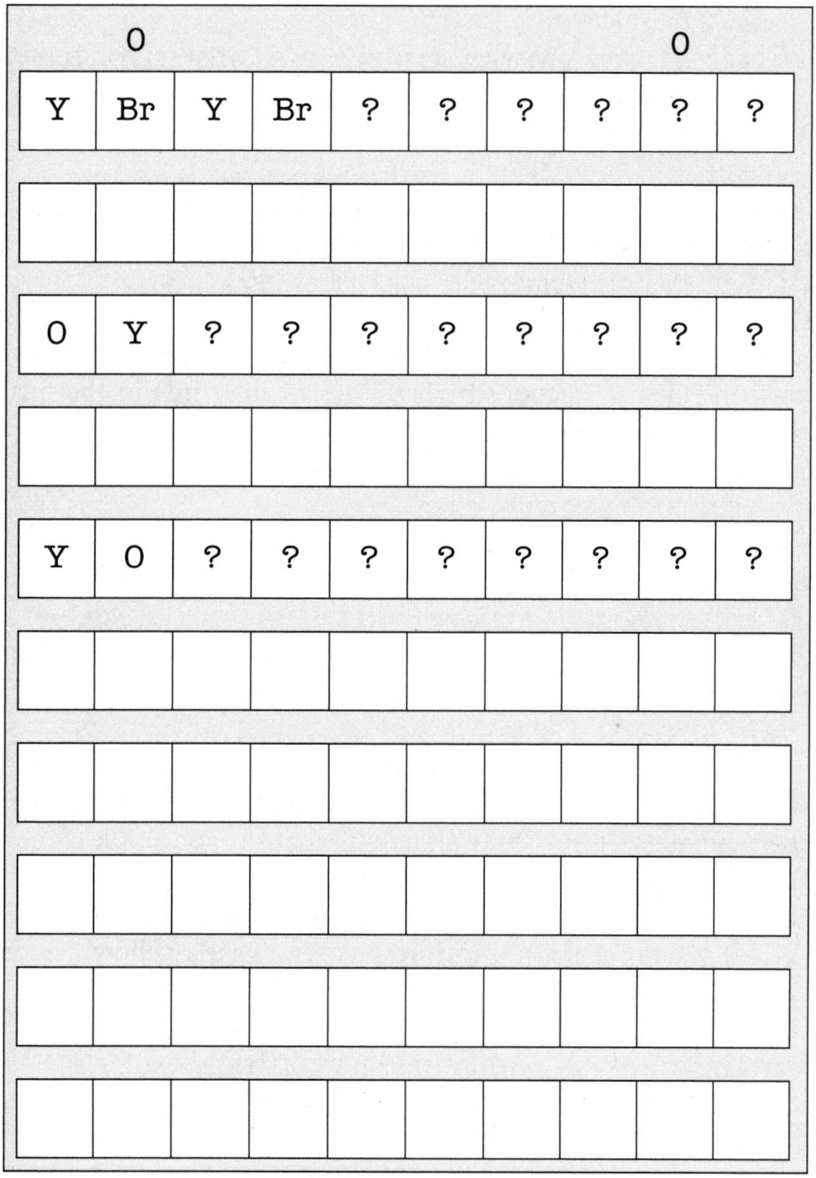

	O							O	
Y	Br	Y	Br	?	?	?	?	?	?

O	Y	?	?	?	?	?	?	?	?

Y	O	?	?	?	?	?	?	?	?

FIGURE 1.4 A pattern pocket chart

RORY: I just know.

BECKY: [*Pointing to the second question mark*] WHAT DO YOU THINK IS HERE?

JAMAL: Brown.

BECKY: HOW DO YOU KNOW?

JAMAL: I see the yellow, brown, yellow, brown pattern.

BECKY: YOU'RE MAKING PREDICTIONS AND THEY'RE COMING TRUE. [*She reveals the yellow and brown cards.*]

The children predict the next colors in unison, and Becky confirms their predictions by revealing all the cards in the first row. She then focuses their attention on the next pattern.

BEN: I think orange is next.

BECKY: DO YOU ALL AGREE WITH BEN?

EVERYONE: Yes.

BECKY: [*Revealing a yellow square*] THIS TIME YOUR PREDICTION DIDN'T COME TRUE.

SAMMY: It'll go orange, yellow, yellow, orange, yellow, yellow.

The children take turns predicting the color of the next square until all of the squares in this row are revealed. Then Becky directs their attention to the third pattern: "What do you think comes next?"

Most of the children predict orange, following the same A–B–B pattern of the previous row. A few suggest yellow. Becky reveals a brown square.

BECKY: WHY DIDN'T ANYBODY THINK IT WOULD BE BROWN?

EZRA: Because it wasn't part of the pattern.

BECKY: YES, IT WASN'T PART OF THE PATTERN UNTIL WE SAW THIS ONE.

Becky then organizes children for the next activity. Once again, they will make patterns with Unifix cubes, teddy bear counters, pattern blocks, and color tiles. The children are now able to pursue these activities on their own, so Becky may work with a group while they do so. Because the game What Comes Next? has the potential to deepen and broaden the children's thinking about patterns, Becky wants the children to play it many times, but not always as a whole class. She invites eight children to learn a version of the game that they can play independently, without the pocket chart. (See Eston and Economopoulos 1998, p. 28, for a complete discussion of this game.)

Becky takes the small group of children to a nearby table, on which she has laid out four color tiles in a row, followed by four small cups turned upside down, each of which has a tile underneath it.

She asks the children to predict the color of tile under the first cup. After several children make predictions, she turns over that cup to reveal the color, much as she did with the pocket chart. The process continues until all the tiles have been revealed.

Becky then asks Lisa and Orin to play the game. Orin covers his eyes while Lisa makes a pattern, hiding the last four tiles under the cups. Orin predicts what comes next. When their game is completed, she asks the other children to tell how the game is played. Once Becky is sure everyone understands what to do, the children pair off and she gives each pair four cups.

As the children play the game, Becky observes. She notes the type of patterns the children make, the language they use to describe their patterns, their ability to predict what comes next, and the basis of their decisions. Through experience, she knows that she does not have to teach all of the children this version of What Comes Next? They will share the game among themselves naturally; it will become a favorite activity during their free-choice explorations. Thinking ahead to next week, Becky decides the children are ready to begin to record their patterns.

Challenges of Teaching in Idea-Centered Classrooms

Becky did not always teach this way. Many years of reflecting on her teaching, enrolling in professional development seminars, and reading teacher-resource books and articles have helped her understand better how to nurture the growth of mathematical ideas. When she first started moving away from focusing on skills and began focusing on ideas, many challenges emerged. Skills are easily identified, described, and recognized. Ideas are broader and more ambiguous. What she was supposed to do became less clear, and the decisions she needed to make became more complex. She remembers thinking, Can I really do this?

There were times when she felt confused and lacked confidence. Somehow various aspects of her teaching were not functioning in concert with one another; she felt uncertain. For example:

- A long-standing favorite counting activity suddenly seemed less appropriate as she embraced the development of meaningful ideas rather than the acquisition of rote skills. Something she always enjoyed no longer matched what she valued in teaching mathematics.
- She had a boy in her classroom who was painfully shy. She wanted all of her students to talk about their mathematical thinking, to share their ideas with one another. How could she encourage that boy to participate without making him uncomfortable?
- She was committed to the development of mathematical ideas but wasn't sure she would be supported by colleagues or administrators. Was her philosophy shared? How could she broach this conversation with the other kindergarten teachers?

Becky's greatest challenge revolved around her role as an "arbitrator of correctness." What was she to say when a child asked, *Is this right?* She became more conscious of the fact that ideas are refined through additional experiences, not through teacher judgment. She began to respond, *What do you think?* or *What could you do to find out?* Sometimes she suggested that a child seeking confirmation confer with a peer. She tried to build autonomy, to encourage students not to depend on her. Sometimes, however, students needed to know their thinking was correct in order to feel safe enough to proceed or to achieve closure. What was she to do then? She began to direct her decision making by asking, *What action will best foster the building of mathematical ideas for this student right now?* She still uses this question to help her make decisions.

Then there was the challenge of time. It takes time to develop ideas that broaden the vision of mathematics and provide children with the ability to understand mathematics. It takes much less time to complete a worksheet that requires only the recall of rote skills than it does to investigate the number of buttons in the classroom. Where was Becky going to find the time to teach this way?

As she continued to explore this approach, she found that time spent ensuring that children understood what they were learning meant she had to spend less time reteaching skills that had been lost because they were not understood or could not be recalled. She found that some of the goals of the literacy, science, and social studies programs could be accomplished within time allotted to mathematics. Similarly, mathematical goals could be accomplished as part of activities from other disciplines. As she began to treasure mathematical investigations, she found some other activities less important and was willing to spend less time on them.

Becky finds the time she needs. She is firmly committed to spending an average of thirty minutes a day on mathematics, not including other daily routines and interdisciplinary connections. She knows that some kindergarten teachers do not designate any time for focused instruction on mathematics, do not begin mathematics instruction until late in October, or do not provide more than ten minutes of mathematical experiences a day. When they ask Becky how she can devote so much time to mathematics, she thinks, How can you not? Once again, her decision is based on what is needed to build mathematical ideas. She is confident in her decision.

Challenges remain, however. For example, Becky continues to struggle with questions like:

- How much knowledge can children construct without her intervention?
- How much frustration can children experience before their curiosity is thwarted?
- How much assistance can she give before children no longer think for themselves?

Over time she has learned that there is never only one response that will foster the growth of ideas. What is important is to be aware of the choices she makes and the information she uses to inform those choices. Sometimes she will make inappropriate choices. If she reflects on her decisions and recognizes those that did not foster the growth of ideas, she is less likely to repeat those errors. Since new situations arise constantly, however, she can never eliminate errors of judgment. She has learned not to be too self-critical, to remind herself that the constant newness is one of the challenges she likes best about teaching.

Establishing a Classroom That Promotes Mathematical Thinking

We all want children to be at home in their classroom. We want them to feel secure, be able to take care of themselves, respect others, and participate as a community of learners. Secure and autonomous children are able to participate more fully than children limited by feelings of insecurity or by an overdependence on others. As instruction moves from simple, rote exercises to more in-depth mathematical investigations, the ability to work within a community and a willingness to take risks become more important. The physical arrangement of Becky's room, the daily routines she creates, and the classroom expectations she establishes are based on her goal of building her students' sense of security, autonomy, and community, each of which supports learning.

Each September Becky thinks about how she will create a classroom for her new students that promotes learning. In order to accomplish all of her goals, the many aspects of her classroom must work in concert. As Becky makes decisions about how she will set up her classroom, one of the factors she thinks about is mathematics. Her goal is to tap students' natural curiosity and spark interest in learning mathematics each day. She wants to take every opportunity to integrate mathematics into daily activities in a meaningful way, to make mathematics come alive in her classroom from the first day of school.

Arranging the Space

When the children walk into their new classroom for the first time, Becky wants them to feel welcomed, safe, and curious about their new home. She wants them to enter a room that presents exciting possibilities, that invites them to learn. Although Becky's classroom changes in small ways throughout the year, its basic structure remains the same.

This overall structure includes five major learning areas: an art center, a technology center, a math/science center, an area for dramatic play, and a meeting space. The physical boundaries of these areas and the way they are used are often more fluid than their discrete labels imply; however, the labels help children develop a conceptual map of their classroom. This helps them navigate the room independently and thus take greater advantage of activities that promote learning. Each area of the room supports mathematical thinking in some manner. (Figure 2.1 shows the physical layout of Becky's classroom.)

Two thirds of Becky's classroom is carpeted, the rest is not. As a matter of practicality, the art center is located in the area with vinyl flooring. A sink, two tables, a painting easel, and art supplies are located there. Becky's students are given countless opportunities to draw, paint, cut, paste, trace, and design. Artwork undertaken during free-choice explorations often embraces mathematical ideas. For example, on Kaitlin's fifth birthday, which she celebrated during the first week of school, she made the drawing shown in Figure 2.2. The following week, Ben traced shape templates to create a house (see Figure 2.3). The sand table is also in this area, and the measuring and mixing for cooking projects takes place here as well. Since many of the art supplies are also used as writing tools, and drawing and writing are so intricately linked at this age, the area also serves literacy

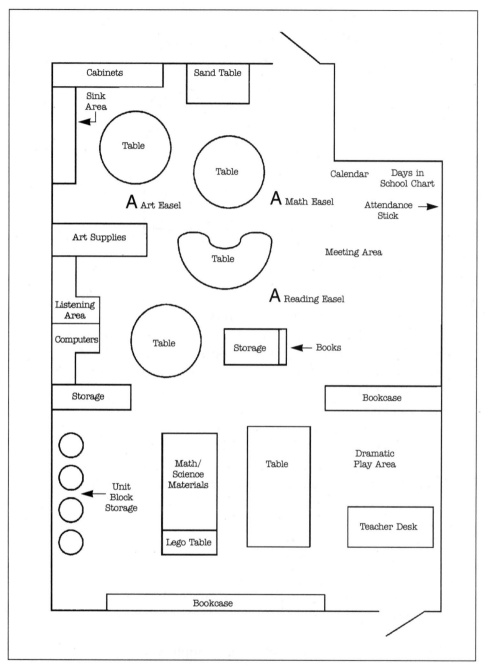

FIGURE 2.1 The physical layout of Becky's classroom

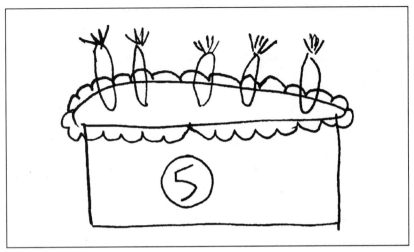

FIGURE 2.2 Kaitlin's drawing of her birthday cake

development. However, it is easier for children to refer to an art center than to an art/cooking/sand/literacy corner!

A listening area containing cozy couches, a tape recorder with headphones, and books on tape bridges the art and technology centers. In the technology center are two computers. Software programs that support the development of number and spatial sense are available.

An area for unit, Duplo, and Lego blocks links the technology center to the math/science center. Playing with blocks helps children develop their sense of three-dimensional geometry and spatial relationships. Often the children's conversations reflect their growing understanding of mathematical terms and ideas:

MARIO: My tower is taller than your tower.

KIMI: Yeah, but mine is bigger.

BECKY: CAN THIS BE TRUE?

JAMAL: Mario's tower is almost as tall as me, but Kimi's tower has more blocks.

A conversation like this helps children grapple with what *big* means and introduces the idea that height and number are distinct attributes.

Kindergartners should have ample opportunity to use blocks and other manipulatives. They need a variety of concrete materials

FIGURE 2.3 Ben's house, which he created by tracing shape templates

to support their hands-on exploration of mathematical ideas. Becky stores all the math manipulatives near the unit blocks; that way, the children see that math manipulatives are as integral a component of the classroom as the more familiar unit blocks are. The manipulatives are housed in plastic tubs so that children can easily carry them to other work areas. The following materials are available to Becky's students at all times; they are mainstays in the classroom, just like pencils, paper, and crayons:

Attribute blocks	Multilink cubes
Balance scales	Parquetry blocks
Buttons	Pattern blocks
Color tiles	Stones
Cuisenaire rods	Straws
Dice	Tangrams
Geoboards	Teddy bear counters
Geoblocks	Two-color counters
Keys	Unifix cubes
Measuring tapes	

A dramatic-play area is adjacent to the math/science center. The initial theme of the year is *house*. There are miniature models of a stove, refrigerator, and sink, along with dress-up clothes and dolls. Dramatic play often reveals how mathematics is used in the children's homes. Overhearing conversations like this one, Becky learns a little more about the children and their families:

HALEY: Let's make soup.

MEGAN: We can make it for our whole family. You make the soup and, Charlie, you set the table.

CHARLIE: How many people do you have in your family?

HALEY: I have four, John, me, and my mom and dad.

MEGAN: I have two, Mom and me.

CHARLIE: I have more than that, Jamie, Michelle, Christopher, Nina, my grandpa and grandma, Mommy and sometimes Daddy.

MEGAN: All those people live at your house? You must have a big house.

CHARLIE: No, just a ton of people.

HALEY: Let's make the soup now.

CHARLIE: How many bowls should I get?

MEGAN: Let's just make us the family. One [*pointing to Charlie*], two [*pointing to Haley*], and me [*pointing to herself and giggling*]. That's three. Hey, *me* and *three* rhyme!

CHARLIE: Okay, here's three bowls and three spoons. Is the soup ready yet? I'm hungry!

The dramatic-play area adjoins the meeting area. In addition to being an open work space, the meeting area is large enough for Becky and all the children to gather and sit comfortably in a circle. It is here that stories are shared and community discussions take place. Before long, these discussions will include the debriefing of mathematical activities.

When Becky first set up her room, she placed an easel in the meeting area and used it to store and display big books and charts. This easel has become a permanent fixture and provides a focal point for shared reading or singing. Finding that the easel served literacy learning so well, Becky set up another easel in the same area for mathematics. It allows her to present engaging problems and questions in large-print format and to record ideas generated in introductory and debriefing discussions. Becky also often displays a flannel board on the math easel. Large flannel representations of objects allow Becky to model (and her students to visualize) how materials can be manipulated. The enlarged-print problems and flannel pieces engage children in the learning process and link literacy and mathematics.

In between the meeting area and the dramatic-play area is the classroom library. At the start of the year, certain books in the library are placed with their covers facing out, because emergent readers often depend on a picture to find out what a book is about. Becky makes sure that several counting books are prominent, perhaps *Counting Wildflowers* (McMillan 1986), *The Very Hungry Caterpillar* (Carle 1989), *Ten Black Dots* (Crews 1986), and *How Many Feet in the Bed?* (Hamm 1991). As children become familiar with various books, the books are placed in bins by topics and placed around the room. The bins have a classification scheme, albeit one constructed by Becky, and children must match individual books to identified categories.

Classification is a thought process that underlies many mathematical ideas, and classification issues often arise in the classroom. For example, in order to count all the doors in the classroom, children must first classify what will be considered a door. One day one of Becky's students, Orin, has been looking through Tana Hoban's book *26 Letters and 99 Cents* (1987). He finishes the book and goes to return it to the bin. He walks toward the bin of alphabet books and starts to replace the book. Then he takes the book back and walks toward the bin of counting books. He hesitates and then finally goes to find Becky.

ORIN: There's a problem with this book, Miss Eston.

BECKY: WHAT'S THE PROBLEM?

ORIN: Well, it's an alphabet book so it goes in the alphabet bin. It's a number book, so it goes in the counting bin.

BECKY: WHAT DO YOU THINK WE SHOULD DO ABOUT THIS?

ORIN: I think we should put this in the counting bin. Then we should buy another one and keep it in the alphabet bin.

BECKY: WE DON'T HAVE MONEY TO BUY ANOTHER ONE. DO YOU HAVE ANY OTHER IDEAS?

ORIN: Maybe we could take turns.

BECKY: WHAT DO YOU MEAN?

ORIN: Well, one week it would be counting and the next it would be alphabet.

BECKY: INTERESTING. IS THERE ANYTHING ELSE WE COULD DO?

ORIN: Well, we could put these two bins next to each other and put the book in the middle.

Orin's intuition has prompted him to explore how sets of books can intersect. He is trying to resolve the conflict he perceives between the way the bins have been set up and the nature of this particular book: the book belongs in both bins. Simple, everyday problems like this capture children's interest and can provide starting points for mathematical experiences.

Tables and chairs are placed strategically in the classroom so that children have ample space in which to do their work. Bulletin boards line some of the classroom walls and are ideal places to display curriculum-related posters and materials. At least half of what Becky displays there is student work, because she wants to demonstrate that their work is valued. Children's mathematical representations often figure prominently in these displays. The children are always proud to have their work exhibited. Sharing work in this way promotes self-confidence, and children broaden their own ideas as they view the work of peers.

Over the years the arrangement of Becky's classroom has changed as she explored new concepts and ideas or new resources became available. As teachers, it's important that we periodically reflect on the arrangement of our classroom. It only takes a few minutes to consider whether it:

- Supports children's ability to find, transport, and use materials easily.
- Provides cozy, private spaces as well as large areas where children can build, sort, experiment, and construct.
- Celebrates children and their work.
- Matches our current philosophy of teaching and learning.

Classroom Routines

Obviously, the physical environment is only one aspect of a classroom that fosters the growth of mathematical ideas. What else does Becky do during the first few weeks of school to promote an investigative approach to mathematics among a community of learners? What happens when the children enter their new classroom?

Becky's primary goal for the first few days of school is to help the children feel comfortable with one another and with her, to transform a group of strangers into a community of learners. The children are not the only ones who experience apprehension and excitement. Becky too wonders what this year will bring, how they will all get along, what the special challenges of this year's group will be. The first-day jitters of both teacher and students settle as they learn about one another and begin to form ways of living together in the classroom. Learning names (a first step in getting to know one another) and establishing basic classroom routines and expectations, therefore, are Becky's focus these first few days, but at the same time she wants to advance her goals for mathematics.

Becky begins to establish daily routines on the first day of school. These routines have been a part of her classroom for many years. Many of them are described in greater detail in the kindergarten units of Investigations in Number, Data and Space (Economopolous et al. 1998; Economopolous and Murray 1998; Economopolous and Russell 1998; Eston and Economopolous 1998; Kilman et al. 1998; Murray et al. 1998). Becky's classroom served as a research site for these six units.

Many teachers begin the day with attendance and calendar routines. Becky has thought about how best to use these traditional routines to support the growth of mathematical ideas in her students and to lay a foundation for a great deal of later learning. For example, taking attendance can be tedious, but it needs to be done. Becky sees taking attendance as a daily opportunity for the children to count and to collect and interpret data. It is also a way to emphasize that it matters who is present each day and that each child is an important member of the classroom learning team.

Attendance Tags

To take attendance, Becky uses a procedure suggested to her several years ago by a colleague, Carolyn Casey. She writes the first name of each child on a tag, punches a hole in the tag, and puts it on a book or shower-curtain ring. As the year progresses a last-name tag is added to the ring, and later an address tag and a telephone-number tag are included as well. These identifying kinds of information give children a sense of personal information, emphasize that there are important numbers in life, and help the children memorize crucial information. As children enter the classroom they put their "attendance tags" in a bucket to signal that they are present. (Some teachers ask each child to bring a photograph from home to place on the ring—the picture allows children who do not recognize their name to find their tag independently.)

As the children enter the classroom on the second day of school, Becky directs them to a table on which she has placed their new attendance tags and a bucket.

BECKY: WELCOME. I HAVE SOMETHING ON THIS TABLE FOR YOU TO LOOK AT. SEE IF YOU CAN FIND YOUR NAME.

MARIO: There are a lot of tags here.

BECKY: WHAT COULD YOU DO TO HELP YOU FIND YOURS?

ROSITA: I could look for Rs.

MEI: I'm going to look for short names.

JOSÉ: I see mine.

MARIO: I need some help.

Each child is acknowledged for finding his or her name, with or without help, and asked to put the tag in the bucket. Since the children enter the classroom over a period of time (about ten minutes or so), Becky can help someone find her or his tag without making other children wait while she does so.

After all the children have found their tag and put it in the bucket, Becky asks everyone to go to the meeting area and look at a book or try a jigsaw puzzle. She wants them to learn right away how to occupy themselves in a purposeful, engaging way while she works with other children, since working with small groups is an essential aspect of her teaching. These first few minutes of the day are an easy time in which students can begin to learn this expectation.

After the children have made the transition from home to school and settled into the school day, Becky holds a class meeting. The children and Becky sit in a circle. It is important to Becky that children learn to be comfortable in large groups, and she has found that sitting in a circle helps everyone feel part of the classroom community. Once Becky is sure that everyone can see everyone else, she asks, "What was on the table when you came in?" After the children respond, she explains, "Each day one of your jobs will be to put your tag into the bucket so that we know you are here. We'll call this your attendance tag." She pulls a tag out of the bucket, holds it up, and says: "If this is your name, please stand up." After the child stands she asks: "Does anyone remember who this is?" Once the child's name is spoken, she asks the child to come get his or her tag. Becky repeats this action until all the tags have been distributed. Through this process each child begins to develop a one-to-one relationship with his or her tag, and all the children become more familiar with the names of their classmates.

Becky's next goal is to have the children discover how many children are in the class:

BECKY: THE BUCKET IS EMPTY. THAT MEANS EVERYONE IS HERE
          TODAY. HOW CAN WE FIND OUT HOW MANY OF US ARE HERE
          TODAY?

ROSITA: We could line up.

TREVOR: We can count everyone.

BECKY: DOES ANYONE ELSE HAVE IDEAS?

ALLISON: We can all count.

SETH: We can count together. [*The children count in unison
          as Becky points to each child.*]

BECKY: SO HOW MANY CHILDREN ARE HERE TODAY?

EVERYONE: Twenty-three.

BECKY: HOW DO YOU KNOW?

SETH: We counted.

SAMMY: We counted and got twenty-three.

BECKY: TWENTY-THREE IS OUR SPECIAL CLASS NUMBER. WHEN WE
          COUNT AND GET TWENTY-THREE, WE KNOW THAT EVERYONE
          IS HERE.

A couple of days later, Becky helps the children count off one at a time. Most students can count by rote when they start with one, but it is more difficult to count on from numbers other than one. Children who lose track of the counting sequence or who don't count along to themselves often need help remembering the number that comes next. Over time, however, their ability to count around the circle one at a time will improve.

Attendance Stick

On a day during the second week of school when everyone is present, Becky introduces the attendance stick. She brings the attendance bucket to the meeting area and holds up the tags one at a time until they are all redistributed. The children count off and establish that twenty-three children are here. Becky then places a Unifix cube on top of each tag.

BECKY: IF WE PUT ALL OF OUR CUBES TOGETHER IN A STICK, HOW
          MANY CUBES DO YOU THINK WE WOULD HAVE?

LISA: Maybe twenty.

JOSÉ: Twenty-three.

KIMI: About fifteen.

TALI: There's twenty-three because that's our special class number.

BEN: I don't know. Let's count.

Some children apparently recognize that the number of cubes will be the same as the total number of children in the class, while others do not yet make this connection. Becky collects the cubes, one by one, and connects them. As she does, she counts the number of cubes, encouraging the children to count along with her. To further establish the one-to-one correspondence between the children, the tags, and the cubes, she again has the children count in sequence around the circle and then asks them to recount the number of cubes in the stick. Becky then holds up the attendance stick and says "When we are all here, the stick has twenty-three cubes. Remember, twenty-three is our special class number. Each day we can use our attendance stick to help us know how many children are here and how many are absent."

The next day Becky identifies a "daily helper." Once the children have counted around the circle, the helper counts the cubes in the previous day's attendance stick and then removes or adds cubes if necessary so that the number of cubes in the stick matches the number of children present that day. Over time, the children learn that cubes not used in the stick represent the children who are absent. Conversations about how many children are in class and how many are absent introduce the concept of part-whole relationships and give the children a daily opportunity to collect data.

On days when everyone is present, there isn't much to say about the attendance stick. On other days, however, the conversation can be quite lively. For example, in midyear the class is anticipating the arrival of a new student:

BECKY: I HAVE SOME EXCITING NEWS! A BOY NAMED LUKE IS MOVING INTO OUR TOWN, AND HE WILL BECOME A NEW MEMBER OF OUR CLASS. WHAT CAN WE DO TO HELP LUKE FEEL WELCOMED?

KAITLIN: We can say hello to him and tell him our names.

TREVOR: We can ask him to play with the blocks.

MARIO: We need to give him a day on the computers.

JAMAL: We need to make him an attendance tag and give him a cubby.

ALLISON: We have to put another cube on the attendance stick for him.

BECKY: THANK YOU, THOSE ARE ALL GOOD IDEAS. WHY WILL WE NEED TO PUT ANOTHER CUBE ON THE ATTENDANCE STICK FOR HIM?

HALEY: Because he makes one more.

ANA: We will have to change the special class number.

BECKY: WHAT WILL OUR SPECIAL CLASS NUMBER BE?

SAMMY: Twenty-four!

BECKY: DOES EVERYONE AGREE WITH SAMMY? (*Most children nod their head yes.*) SAMMY'S RIGHT, THERE WILL BE TWENTY-FOUR CHILDREN IN OUR CLASS AFTER LUKE MOVES IN. YOU'VE HELPED ME REMEMBER SOME THINGS I WILL NEED TO DO BEFORE HE GETS HERE. I APPRECIATE YOUR HELP.

The next day Luke arrives to find a cubby and attendance tag and lots of new friends. Becky also brings a new cube to add to the attendance stick, just as the children suggested. A few days later Nicole is the daily helper and three children are absent. The conversation during the morning meeting unfolds like this:

BECKY: NICOLE, HOW CAN YOU TELL HOW MANY CHILDREN ARE HERE AND HOW MANY ARE NOT?

NICOLE: I can go look at how many tags are left on the table.

BECKY: OKAY.

NICOLE: [*Walking over to the table and seeing that three tags were not placed in the bucket*] Three. Three children are absent.

BECKY: HOW MANY CHILDREN ARE HERE TODAY?

NICOLE: [*Without hesitation*] Twenty.

BECKY: HOW DID YOU KNOW THAT SO FAST?

NICOLE: Because it's always twenty when three kids are absent.

TALI: No, 'cause now we have Luke. I think it is twenty-one.

SAMMY: I agree with Tali.

NICOLE: Oh, yeah. Sorry, Luke, I forgot about you.

BECKY: HOW CAN WE DOUBLE-CHECK OUR THINKING?

CHARLIE: We can count everybody that is here.

As attendance discussions take place during the year, Becky occasionally prompts, "Is there another way to know how many children are here?" A variety of methods are suggested over time. One child gives each child present a cube, re-collects the cubes to form a stick, and then compares that stick to the attendance stick. Another child says that Sammy was the only one out yesterday and is the only one out again today, so the attendance is the same as yesterday. Through such discussions the children learn that there are a variety of ways to solve mathematical problems and further explore the significance of the one-to-one relationships among themselves, the tags, and the cubes.

Calendar

Calendar activities are part of most kindergarten routines, and they offer wonderful opportunities for mathematical thinking. Becky has fashioned a monthly calendar out of cards that are turned over each day to reveal the date. This allows the children to predict what number comes next. Other teachers may prefer to display all the numbers all month long, in order to give students a sense of an entire month. Both decisions make sense given their purpose.

Some teachers create patterns on their calendars (for example, the dates in May might be alternated on cards shaped as daisies and tulips to establish an A–B pattern). Becky prefers to use the pocket chart described in Chapter 1 to work with such patterns. However, she does encourage children to notice patterns inherent to the calendar, like the fact that there is never school on Saturdays and Sundays.

Every day, after the children have sung a community song about the days in the week, Becky asks the children to predict what that day's date will be. The conversation below takes place on Thursday of a school week that began on Monday, September 6:

CHARLIE: I think it will be nine.

ANA: I think so, too.

BECKY: WHY DO YOU THINK SO?

ALLISON: It's six, seven, eight, nine.

KIMI: It goes one, two, three, four, five, six, seven, eight, nine.

EZRA: Nine is after eight.

Becky turns over the next calendar card to confirm the students' predictions. (Once this routine is established, the daily helper turns the card to reveal the date.) Through this daily activity children see numbers in order, explore how ordinal numbers are used, and are exposed to one way in which time is recorded. They also have the opportunity to try out a variety of counting strategies. They may just know the next number. They may start from one and count all of the cards until they arrive at the unknown number. Like Allison, they may count on from a known number.

Becky uses additional cards, marked with icons and displayed all month long, to call attention to significant dates, and the calendar thus becomes a tool to organize and remember information. For example, in October, a week before the children are to take a field trip to a nearby farm, Becky asks, "How many days until we go to the farm?" It's a difficult question, since the children are not sure which days to count. Should today's day be counted? the day of the trip? only the days in between? As teachers, we need to remember to have our students explain their thinking, not merely respond with an answer. At this age, what is most important is that their reasoning makes sense and corresponds to the answer they've given.

Becky makes a point of building the language of mathematics into her ongoing routines. Conversations like the one below, which is prompted by the fact that it is Monday, December 1, allow children to negotiate meaning, form shared ideas, and learn some conventions for expressing these ideas.

BECKY: WHAT DO YOU NOTICE ABOUT OUR CALENDAR TODAY?

MEI: Today is the first day of the new month.

BEN: It's the first day of the week, too.

ALLISON: Sunday is the first day of the week.

BEN: Saturday and Sunday are not part of the week, they are the weekend.

KAITLIN: Both of the weekends start with S.

ALLISON: Sunday isn't the week*end*, it's the beginning of the week.

SAMMY: It's not the beginning, because it goes in circles.

TANYA: There are seven days in a week.

EZRA: There are five days in a week and two days in the weekend.

Becky is amazed and intrigued by conversations like this. They confirm her belief that children naturally attempt to make sense of things. It is the teacher's role to listen carefully to their thoughts and then decide whether or not to intervene, either by confirming their thinking or by helping them see that their theories may need altering or further development.

In this conversation the children have identified an interesting conflict about what is conventionally called a *week* or a *weekend*. Becky could drastically alter this moment by telling them her understanding of the conventional use of the term *weekend*. She chooses not to, however, because she knows that concepts and ideas are not developed within a single conversation and that cognitive conflicts are not resolved by the teacher's providing clarification. Rather, issues are raised and identified, and over time are resolved. Such discourse, interwoven throughout the day and over the course of the year, is part of the doing of mathematics. One reason Becky uses routines like the calendar is because it gives children repeated opportunities to encounter the same conflicts as well as time to develop and firmly establish their understanding. Next Monday she will ask a question about the beginning of the week to make sure the children return to these ideas.

How Many Days?

Becky also makes a routine of the question *How many days have we been in school?* There is a permanent grid of two-inch squares, ten squares across and eighteen squares down, next to the calendar (see Figure 2.4). Since the spaces are small and many children are not yet able to write numerals, Becky does the recording herself. On the first day she writes "1" in the upper-left square and places one Unifix cube on the chalk tray to link the written symbol to a concrete model. The second day she writes "2" in the square next to the "1" and attaches a second cube to the first.

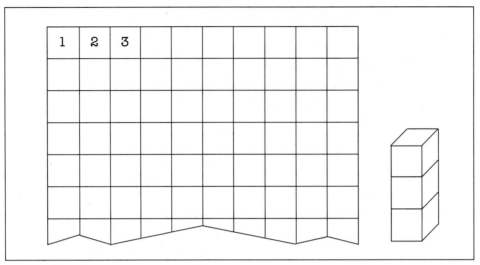

FIGURE 2.4 Two ways of keeping track of the number of school days

(Again, once a daily helper is designated, he or she will add the cube.) Every day for the first three weeks the children orally count the number of cubes as Becky points to them one at a time. After that, although the numeral is written and a cube is attached each day, the children count all of the cubes once a week, then once every two weeks.

Another way to do this activity is to represent the number of school days with a number line that will eventually extend around much of the room. While such a model is appropriate for upper elementary children, it usually doesn't work with children in the primary grades. The number line is more abstract, and the daily number quickly gets too distant from the meeting area. Children this young need models that can easily be seen and touched.

Some kindergarten teachers may prefer not to include a routine that will involve numbers in the hundreds. Becky uses it because she wants to expose her students to these large numbers. Besides, seeing the spaces fill up helps them develop a sense of time, a difficult concept for young children.

The how-many-days routine also poses an interesting problem for the children to solve. When the train of cubes is about thirty cubes long, it becomes difficult to hold together and breaks into pieces. Becky used to organize the cubes in trains of ten, thinking that she was helping children gain a sense of grouping by tens. But she found out that grouping by tens was not significant to the children. Now she simply says, "Hmm, this is frustrating. The train keeps breaking. What should we do?" Suggestions over the years have included:

• "Break the train in half." This prompted a lively discussion about what a half means. Each day the daily helper had to decide which train to place the cube on in order to keep the trains "even." A discussion of even and odd numbers also recurred over many days.

• "Make smaller stacks." This idea comes up often. One year the stacks were groups of two, another year they were groups of four, and still another year they were groups of nine. This confirmed for Becky that her old way of using ten may have been meaningful for her but was as random to the children as two, four, and nine.

• "Let's not use the cubes at all." The children who make this comment are probably letting Becky know that deciding how to organize the cubes is a difficult task that may not be meaningful at this time. However, she does not follow the children's lead in this case, because she feels it is critical to have a physical representation for the numbers on the days-of-school chart. This growing set of cubes often entices children to practice counting on their own. They frequently take a pointer and count the numbers on the chart and the stacks of cubes when they "play school." They also repeat the calendar portion of the morning meeting, just as they read and reread familiar books from shared reading.

While it takes a bit of time to establish all these routines, they proceed quickly once they're up and running. Most mornings, the attendance and calendar routines take about five minutes, although a couple of extra minutes may be needed whenever the month changes or when attendance is unusually low or on days when the cubes are counted. Sometimes Becky is able to anticipate the extra time, sometimes she isn't. Being flexible and following the children's lead is always an important consideration.

Responsibility and Respect

Completing rote exercises on a worksheet requires different behavior from children than when they work together, share materials, and listen to each other as they explain their mathematical thinking. Classroom expectations must be established to support this kind of mathematical work. In Becky's classroom, children share responsibility for communal materials; are responsible for themselves as much as possible, in terms of their physical needs and safety; and are expected to be responsive to the needs of others.

Communal work cans provide easy, readily available access to a few basic materials. On the first day of school the children help Becky fill the cans (empty soup cans work well) for the first time. (By helping, the children become invested in the materials and curious about what they are going to do with them.) Each can gets one primary pencil and one number 2 pencil, a pair of scissors, and a set of eight crayons. The cans are then kept out on top of the storage area in the center of the room, easy to get and put away.

Work cans serve a couple of purposes. First, this basic set of tools gives students enough materials to start any project without being overwhelmed by choices, although the children learn early on that they can always go to the art center for additional materials. Second, the cans are easy to carry around the classroom as the children move from one work area to another.

At the beginning of school many children don't understand the communal nature of these materials. They think the can they filled is theirs. During the first few days of school, Allison looks at the cans quizzically and says, "I can't remember which can is mine." Ben picks up a can and laments, "I don't remember where I wrote my name." When Becky tells them, "The cans belong to everyone; no one has his or her own can," their eyes widen in amazement.

Becky makes it clear from the beginning that she expects the children to share the work cans and also take care of them. Since the cans are used so frequently, it's not long before some have only six crayons and others have ten. Then the children and Becky redistribute the contents. It is clear that many of the children are not used to this level of responsibility, but Becky thinks it is important to include them. First, the task involves sorting, matching, and counting. Then, too, it supports the notion that the materials in the classroom are "ours" and that we all have responsibility for what happens to them. This shared sense of ownership is important in mathematics activities that involve the joint use of manipulatives.

Basic "rules" for classroom behavior support independence and build respect for one another, as well as provide a vehicle through which children can talk about these important goals. Becky teaches in a school that has three basic rules:

- Work hard.
- Play fair.
- Respect one another.

The school's teachers and administrators who worked on these rules thought carefully about what rules were necessary and how to express them. They came up with a minimum number of rules that can be learned by children at all grade levels. Rather than a series of statements that begin with the word *don't*, these rules are positive statements that support the notion that rules are not a list of limitations but instead identify behavior that helps us succeed. The rules are expressed in the school song, written on school folders, and addressed in school meetings. Older brothers and sisters tell them to younger siblings. In this way, a school culture is developed that reinforces the behavioral expectations in every classroom.

Children learn to understand these rules, and the importance of following them, through concrete examples. Management issues are viewed as part of the children's social and intellectual development. Becky asks, "Why do we take down block structures carefully, rather than crashing them?" Noticing a child walking carefully around a block building, Becky says, "I noticed that you walked around Ben's building carefully. That shows respect for Ben's work."

Becky also presents dilemmas to the children so that they can practice making judgments about behavior. For example, one day she tells this story at meeting time:

This is a story about two girls, Chantel and Julia. Chantel was making a pattern with pattern blocks. She had been working on the pattern for some time and it was very beautiful. Julia wanted to use the pattern blocks too. She asked Chantel if she could help. Chantel said, "No, I want to do it myself." Julia got tired of waiting. She walked over to Chantel's pattern and messed it all up. This made Chantel very mad. She turned to Julia and pushed her.

Then Becky prompts the children to identify more appropriate responses by asking, "What could Julia and Chantel do next time this happens? How could this problem have been avoided?"

In addition to making rules concrete, Becky uses her interactions with the children to make it clear how she expects them to behave. During the first few days of school, children are constantly asking for Becky's assistance. On the way out to recess Tanya says, "My sweater is inside out." Becky replies, "Watch me do one sleeve, then I'll watch you do the other." During snack time Rory asks, "Will you please help me open my granola bar?" Becky responds, "If you get a work can, I'll show you how you can do it yourself," then asks him to take out the scissors and cut off the end of the wrapper. Once Rory has succeeded, Becky tells him that tomorrow he can get the can without asking and do it himself. Rory is beaming.

In the short term, it would be much quicker for Becky to simply fix the sweater and pull open the wrapper herself. In fact, to an uninitiated observer it looks like a great deal of Becky's time is spent with these minilessons. Before long, however, the children become more independent, and Becky spends less and less time on such activities. More important, the children are learning that they can rely on themselves. If they can't depend on themselves to fix their sweater, how can she ask them to trust their own mathematical thinking?

Cleaning Up and Ending the Day

Cleaning up is both a daily routine and an expectation. Because the centers in the classroom are communal space and all materials are shared, daily cleanup is a community effort. All items in the classroom must be put away or saved in some manner for tomorrow's use. Tables must be cleared and cleaned, computers need to be shut down, and the tape recorder in the listening center has to be turned off. Children begin cleaning wherever they are working at the end of the day, and when they finish, they are expected to find another area that needs their help. If students seem hesitant about identifying a second area to help clean, Becky prompts them with a question like *Did you use the unit blocks today?* It is important for everyone to feel responsible for the classroom as a whole.

Each day has its own rhythm, but just as the day begins with a meeting to establish community, it also ends with one. The children use this time to think about the school day they've just completed. Becky uses questions like these to get them started:

- What is something you did today that made you proud?
- What is one thing you learned in math today?
- How many of you did something today you've never done before?
- Does anyone have a compliment to share?

This final daily routine demonstrates the importance of reflective thinking. Following this discussion there is usually time for a community song or story, providing a calm and orderly end to the day.

Throughout these early days the children learn about one another and their new classroom. They begin to anticipate what will happen each day, to form expectations for learning, to build relationships with each other and with Becky, and to become more independent. Within a couple of weeks they will recognize and predict the routines; they will have gained a sense of security, autonomy, and community that will support their learning of mathematical ideas.

3

Making Plans for Teaching and Learning Mathematics

Noted mathematics educator Glenda Lappan (1993) describes teachers as architects, as designers of the curriculum. A professional architect envisions and designs buildings, chooses the materials that will be used to construct those buildings, and supervises the building process. As curriculum architects, teachers choose the type of mathematical ideas they will emphasize in their classroom. They decide on activities that will build their students' understanding of mathematics and determine how those activities will be linked. They guide children's explorations and, in general, decide how much time will be spent on the development of mathematical thinking.

Not all teachers view being a curriculum designer as one of their primary roles. Some kindergarten teachers focus exclusively on developing a child-centered environment within which the children's intrinsic motivation, interests, and initiative dictate the activities. In such classrooms, there is minimal intervention from teachers. These teachers argue that it is more important to nurture children's independence, creativity, and self-esteem than it is to provide them with teacher-guided activities designed to challenge cognitive development.

But such a separation of goals is unnecessary. If teachers are able to develop children's ability to do mathematics, they will simultaneously nurture children's independence, creativity, and self-esteem. To that end, all teachers need to plan meaningful mathematical experiences for their students.

Part of planning is to construct a daily schedule that balances all the important aspects of learning that need to be addressed. This is no easy charge; demands on teachers and expectations for student learning continue to increase, even in kindergarten. As Becky plans each year, she does so from two perspectives: her overall goals, and the activities she will offer her students day by day. She wants to provide a structure for learning that is both consistent and flexible. She thinks about how learning develops and the systems she needs to have in place so that all her students will be successful.

In her classroom Becky uses three basic formats: *explorations*, *workshops*, and *meetings*. She helps the children understand the nature of these formats by discussing them explicitly.

During an *exploration*, children have a free choice among activities, and all the centers are available. Being allowed to make their own choices helps them gain confidence in their ability to make appropriate decisions and to take responsibility for doing so. (Becky uses the term *exploration* rather than *free choice* because she thinks it better describes the purposefulness of children's play.)

During a *workshop*, all the children work on an activity initiated by Becky. Sometimes they all pursue the same investigation, sometimes children may choose from a number of designated tasks. Although Becky provides the general outline for a workshop activity, the children may often choose whether to work on their own, with a partner, or in a small group. They are also often encouraged to choose the materials they wish to use.

A *meeting* can incorporate a variety of shared activities. As we've seen, a day in Becky's classroom starts and ends with a meeting intended to develop a sense of community and to set out or review the events of the day. There may be additional meetings throughout the day in which a new topic is introduced or in which some children share their work while the rest of the class participates as an audience. Following a workshop, the class may return to the meeting area in order to discuss and reflect on new learning. Occasionally, Becky has brief meetings between activities in which the children sing together, listen to a story, or participate in a shared reading.

Together these three types of activities provide a balance of child-initiated play and structured investigations. They also give children experience working alone, in pairs, in small groups, and as a whole class. Each day, Becky posts a schedule of the day's events for the children to look at; periodically, she reviews the list with them so that they can anticipate what will happen next.

Because Becky uses these terms consistently, her students understand what is expected of them throughout the day. But Becky also wants parents and guardians to understand these different learning formats; when they do, they can better communicate with the children about their day at school. Here's part of a newsletter she sends home in which she explains her three instructional vehicles:

Room 103 News!

September 19

Dear Families,

Our days in kindergarten continue to be very full! Your child has probably already begun talking about various aspects of our school day, using the words *exploration*, *workshop*, and *meeting* when telling you about daily events. Children choose their own activities during an *exploration*, while in *workshops* they investigate tasks that I introduce and oversee. During *meetings* we come together as a community to sing, read, and share ideas. I believe that using these terms helps children focus on the important work that we do each day.

I have elected to use these words consistently so that I will be able to foster a spirit of investigation regardless of the subject matter being considered. Setting up our daily activities under these three umbrellas encourages cooperative play and social development. Working together is a vital part of kindergarten.

As the year progresses, you will see that the children will constantly be using their emerging reading and writing skills as they engage in mathematical and scientific inquiry. . . .

Workshops and explorations are often combined. A small group may work with Becky in a workshop while other children pursue their own explorations. (All the children have the opportunity to participate in the workshop activity within a two-day span.) Other times the whole class does a workshop activity at the same time, working in small groups. Becky selects the format that best supports the task at hand.

Workshops are occasionally designated writing, reading, science, or math workshops, as appropriate. By making these additional identifications, Becky clues the children into expected outcomes and behavior.

Math Workshop

Within the first few days of school, Becky introduces the whole class to some of the mathematics materials in the room and sets in motion what will take place in math workshop.

BECKY: WE'RE GOING TO HAVE A MATH WORKSHOP. WHAT DO YOU THINK THAT IS?

ANA: When you do math.

BECKY: WHAT IS MATH?

LISA: It's like what is three plus two.

BECKY: IS THAT ALL MATH IS?

JOSÉ: Sometimes math is building.

Becky records on the math easel the key words the children use to describe mathematics. She tells them, "Today we're going to look at new materials." She has set up a number of separate work areas and supplied each of them with one of four materials—teddy bear counters, Unifix cubes, pattern blocks, and Cuisenaire rods. Then she divides the class into groups, three or four children in a group. The children spend about ten minutes with one material and then move on to spend ten minutes with a second material.

Becky moves among the groups and records her observations. She will reread these notations at the end of the day as a way to reflect on her new students. She will also refer to these notes over time to help her recognize similarities and changes in the children's work. She pays attention to how the groups function, any mathematical vocabulary the children use, and what they do with the materials. She has developed a series of questions over the years that she keeps in mind to help target her observations:

- How do the children work, alone or with others?
- Do they share materials and ideas?
- Do they notice the work of others? build on others' work?
- Do they place materials flat, on edge, or in stacks?
- Do they make patterns or designs?
- Do they count, group, or order the materials?
- How do they describe their work? Do they use any standard mathematical terms? create their own descriptive terms?

Today the children in one of the groups make trains with the Unifix cubes and then attempt to count the number of cubes they've used. Becky smiles to herself at this typical response. Charlie, Seth, and Ana decide to connect their individual trains to make a longer train.

At the pattern block table Lisa, Tali, and Trevor are making geometric designs, while Tanya and Orin are making patterns in a line. The children work separately but pay attention to one another's products. Becky notes that they refer to *squares* and *triangles* but describe the yellow hexagon shapes and red trapezoid shapes by color.

Most children build vertically with the Cuisenaire rods. Many cross the rods, much as they would assemble Lincoln Logs. Becky watches Allison build a staircase and Seth sort his rods, placing all like rods in the same pile. Becky used to believe that children who sorted this way were paying attention to length, but she has learned that this is not necessarily the case. To find out what criterion Seth is using, she points to a rod and asks, "Why did you put this rod here?" Seth responds, "It's blue."

The teddy bear counters lend themselves to more dramatic play. Kimi forms two lines of bears and talks about her "bear teams." She takes the bear from the end of each line and moves it to the front. Then she gets the next two bears and moves them up for their "turns." Charlie mimics Kimi's motions. José makes concentric circles of bears and counts the number of bears in each circle several times. Mario talks about his "bear family" and tells everyone that there are four bears in his family. He asks the other children, "How many bears are in your family?"

The children are beginning to work together, to become familiar with these materials, and to gain a sense of what will happen during math workshop. After each group of children have explored two materials, Becky convenes a class meeting. She writes *Math Workshop* on the math easel, then points to *Math* and asks, "Does anyone know what this says?" Once the children have identified the word, Becky prompts them to talk about the explorations they've just finished.

BECKY: WHO CAN SHARE SOMETHING YOU DID IN MATH WORKSHOP?

KAITLIN: I built a train.

BEN: I built a tower.

RORY: I counted my bears.

EZRA: I measured with the cubes.

BECKY: IS THERE ANYTHING ELSE YOU DID?

ALLISON: I used my imagination.

Becky again records key words from their responses. Having children talk as a group about what they do each day helps them identify the important aspects of their work. This debriefing is an essential part of instruction. It encourages children to reflect on the mathematics they do, to identify the big ideas, to make sense of these ideas, and to learn from others. Through their discussion today the children have gained a clear view of the type of activities that occur during math workshop. Their view of mathematics has already broadened.

Throughout the week the children explore additional materials and have similar reflective conversations. The list of the kinds of things they do or work on in math workshop is permanently posted in the meeting area and referred to throughout the year. By midyear the list is much longer and contains a greater variety of ideas (see Figure 3.1). While the children cannot read the list independently, they know it is growing and with repeated exposure, learn to recognize some of the terms.

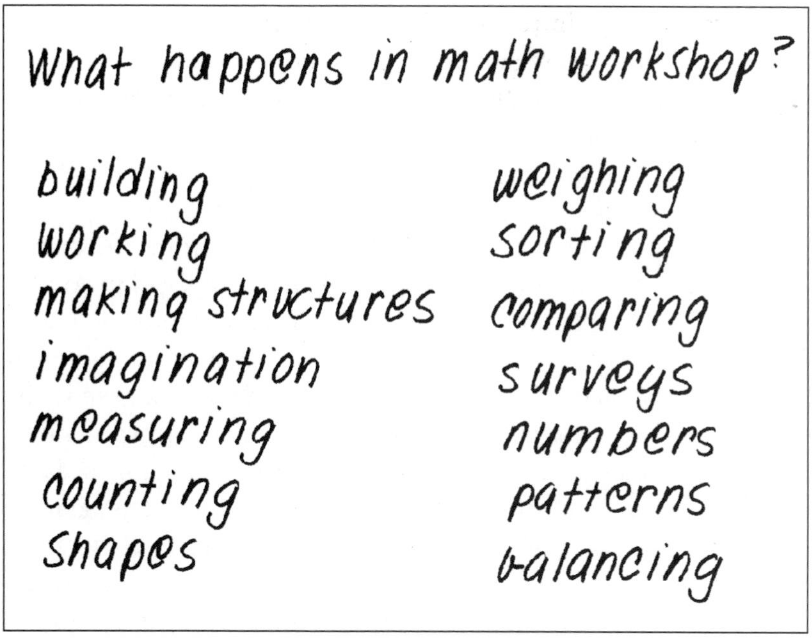

What happens in math workshop?

building   weighing
working   sorting
making structures   comparing
imagination   surveys
measuring   numbers
counting   patterns
shapes   balancing

FIGURE 3.1   The growing list of math activities

Linking Math Workshops

As important as it is for Becky to structure each daily math work-shop, this is only a small piece of the puzzle. Connecting one workshop to another is the next step. Children do not acquire an important mathematical idea in a single workshop. Such ideas build day after day and must then be revisited throughout the year to make sure that they continue to flourish. Therefore Becky tries to link the activities she presents in workshops into se-quences that are connected and interwoven.

Thinking about the importance of linking workshops changes the framework for teacher planning. The question *What would be a good activity for tomorrow?* becomes *What did we do today that should be developed further tomorrow?* Through such analysis Becky is able to link activities by design rather than by default. Once these links have been established in her own mind, she wants to help the children make the links as well.

Becky often begins a new workshop by asking, "Who can tell me what we did yesterday in math workshop?" The children's responses allow her to introduce the next activity in relationship to the work of the previous day. For example, "Yesterday we made patterns with Unifix cubes. Today we are going to make patterns again, but this time with color tiles." Not only does such an introduction help link the two days, but the children understand immediately what they are going to do today.

Becky also uses children's work as a bridge from one day to the next. For example, one day the children are engaged in sorting activities. Most of the groups sort their objects by color or shape, but Ana and Lisa are sorting shells by size. After deciding which shells are small and which are large, they decide to place the shells in order. Ana is certain the shells should be ordered from small to large, and Lisa is just as certain they should be ordered from large to small. Since they cannot agree, they decide to sort separately. Each child places a quantity of shells in order according to her preference. Becky puts their work, along with the work of some other children, on trays and brings the trays to a meeting the next day.

BECKY: I HAVE SOME WORK FROM YESTERDAY THAT I WANT YOU ALL TO SEE. [*She invites Charlie and Megan to show the tiles they sorted by color and Nicole and Trevor to show the wooden pieces they sorted by shape. Next she calls on Ana and Lisa.*] ANA AND LISA, WILL YOU TELL US WHAT YOU DID WITH YOUR SHELLS?

ANA: I put them from little to big.

LISA: Mine go from big to little.

BECKY: CAN YOU TELL US WHY YOU WORKED SEPARATELY?

LISA: 'Cause they're different.

ANA: We couldn't agree on the way to go. I want little to big.

JOSÉ: But you can still put them together.

BECKY: CAN YOU TELL US MORE, JOSÉ?

JOSÉ: It depends on which way you look at them.

BECKY: DOES ANYONE ELSE THINK IT MATTERS WHICH WAY YOU LOOK AT THE SHELLS?

TANYA: [*Who is sitting directly across from Ana's collection*] From here, Ana's shells look big to little.

The children take turns looking at the shell collections from the front and from the back. They discover that the order looks different, depending on the side from which the shells are viewed. Ana and Lisa are happy to discover that they can put their shells together to form one group, and still allow Ana to view them from little to big and Lisa to view them from big to little. During the math workshop that follows, many children order objects according to size. The discussion has informed Ana's and Lisa's work as well as broadened the thinking of other children.

Sharing ideas is another way to link activities. As she did in the discussion about what happens in math workshop, Becky often records the children's ideas on the math easel. These notations are a summary of the discussion and can be returned to later. For example, one day two-dimensional shapes are the focus of a discussion. The children's ideas about rectangles, shown in Figure 3.2, do not define all aspects of rectangles. Further,

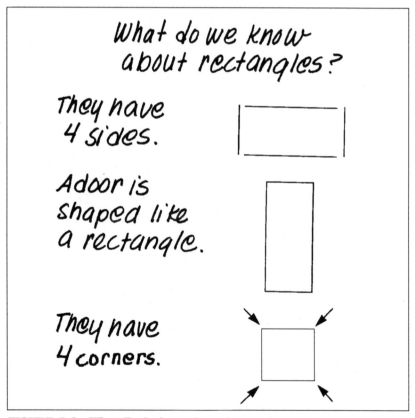

FIGURE 3.2   What Becky's students know about rectangles

although children often refer to a *corner*, the correct term is *vertex*. It is frequently difficult to balance the desire to honor children's thinking and the need for correct mathematics.

But, in kindergarten, children are just beginning to explore the properties of shapes. Becky prefers to use the children's natural language[1] and let them discover the important ideas. Over the years, there will be plenty of time to develop more formal definitions and terms. So Becky keeps this piece of chart paper displayed, and whenever a child is uncertain about whether or not a particular shape is a rectangle, she helps her or him compare the shape to the items on the list.

After Becky's students have discussed an exploration, she uses the following questions to help her plan for the next day:

- What was said that needs further clarification or suggests incomplete understanding?
- What common phrases did children use to describe their work? How can these phrases inform tomorrow's discussions?
- What questions did the children ask or what interests did they identify?
- Did anyone say anything that suggested a developmental level of learning I did not expect? What do I need to do to explore this further?

In thinking about linking one day's work to another, Becky realizes that there is no one best next step. Rather, she concentrates on developing a learning sequence that best fits the needs of the children. Another teacher could listen to the same debriefing conversation and follow up in a different way. Interests and values influence the ways in which we listen and to what we pay attention. What is most important is that teachers think about the possible next steps and find ways to communicate the links to

---

[1] In order to help the emerging readers and the more visually oriented, Becky also includes graphics in her chart summaries. To avoid limiting the children's thinking, she tries to vary the drawings: when representations of two-dimensional figures are too similar, children may assume additional criteria for those figures. For example, many children believe that triangles must be drawn parallel to the bottom of a page or do not realize that squares are also rectangles.

their students. The learning path should be neither accidental nor a secret to the students and their parents.

Linking math workshops has another important aspect as well. Becky also wants children to make connections among the various mathematical content strands. She wants children to know that there are number patterns as well as shape and color patterns. She wants children to develop reasoning and problem-solving skills that cut across the mathematics curriculum. For example, when children are counting a collection of objects to find the total number in the set, they need to find a way to ensure that each one is counted exactly once. The same skill is required when children collect survey data; they need to be sure that each person is surveyed exactly once. When instruction focuses on these organizational strategies and ideas in meaningful ways, children remember the related skills and apply them to new situations.

When Ben and Allison conduct a class survey, they make this type of connection. Let's listen in:

BEN: This makes me angry.
BECKY: WHAT'S THE MATTER, BEN?
BEN: We don't know who we counted.
BECKY: HMM, TELL ME MORE.
ALLISON: We started counting and then we can't remember if we did it twice.
BECKY: WHAT DO YOU WANT TO DO?
BEN: I want to know who we already did.
BECKY: YOU WANT TO KEEP TRACK OF WHO YOU ASKED ALREADY. HOW COULD YOU DO THAT?
BEN: We could make a list.
ALLISON: We could put a sticker on each person.
BEN: Like when we counted the posters in the classroom. Let's do that.

By linking their task to one completed previously, Ben and Allison are able to imagine how this technique will work in the current activity and incorporate it.

Finally, math workshops are linked so that they develop ideas that are the framework of the year's curriculum. As teachers, most of us focus more on short-term planning—that is, we spend most of our time making plans for the next day. Our busy schedules allow for little else. Many of us lament the fact that there never seems to be time for any long-range planning. So while we may try to make links from one day to the next, we rarely seem to have much time to pull back for a broader perspective on the month or the year. Nevertheless, in order to ensure that selected activities provide a curriculum that is comprehensive, balanced, and connected, we need to find a moment every so often to step back and think about the "big picture."

Processes and Content

Becky works in a public school system that has traditionally recognized how important it is for teachers to make decisions about their curriculum. The faculty at her school has spent many hours over many years discussing the content of the mathematics curriculum. At the same time, Becky's principal, Joanne McManus, supports her staff members' professional development. The combination of Becky's participation in ongoing faculty discussions about what mathematics children should learn and in professional development projects and workshops focused on how children learn mathematics is a key factor in her ability to think about her curriculum.

In 1998, in *Principles and Standards for School Mathematics: Discussion Draft*, the National Council of Teachers of Mathematics identified problem solving, reasoning and proof, communication, connection, and representation as "the mathematical processes through which students should acquire and use their mathematical knowledge" (p. 46). In Becky's classroom, these processes serve as integrating threads that weave the curriculum into a holistic plan for instruction.

Problem solving permeates Becky's curriculum. After all, the primary reason to learn mathematics is to be able to use it to solve problems. Intriguing problems provide the context within which mathematical concepts and skills are developed. These problems often arise naturally in the classroom environment. Becky provides the children with ample opportunity to develop their own problem-solving strategies, to pose questions, and to engage in mathematical inquiry. Through such an approach to instruction, her students learn to be confident and independent users of mathematical ideas.

Reasoning and *proof*, in a formal sense, are beyond kindergartners, but Becky believes children at this age are capable of informal reasoning and of forming generalizations. They can explain their thinking, discover relationships, make conjectures, and discover patterns. From many specific examples of the A–B pattern they can generalize that red, blue, red, blue, red, blue is structurally the same as heart, flower, heart, flower, heart, flower. When playing Guess the Label with attribute blocks, they can look at a set of four of the triangular shapes, induce their common structure, and name it. They can recognize basic relationships like the fact that every person has two feet, which is the first tiny step toward proportional reasoning. A curriculum that values reasoning places children in the role of sense maker rather than rule learner and empowers them as mathematical thinkers.

Communication encourages children to articulate, demonstrate, and make more explicit their understanding of mathematical ideas. Children need to discuss, draw, model, dramatize, symbolize, and begin to write about their ideas in order for them to solidify. Children must make connections between natural language and mathematical symbols and relate different representations of mathematical ideas. While working in pairs or small groups and in whole-class discussions, children in Becky's classroom have opportunities to talk about mathematics and to build their mathematical vocabulary. Language helps them mediate their mathematical experiences and gives Becky a window into their thinking.

Connection emphasizes the links and relationships among mathematical topics and between mathematics and other subject areas. For too long mathematics has been taught as a series of discrete, isolated topics. In order for children to view mathematics as a relevant tool in their lives, the curriculum must connect mathematics to the real world. In order to be able to use math's full potential, children must first make generalizations across mathematical topics. Young children need to revisit existing concepts as new ideas emerge, so that they will be better able to nurture relationships among them. That the notion of revisiting ideas is critical to Becky is evident in her daily routines.

Representation of mathematical ideas helps children organize and express their thinking. Becky encourages her students to use objects, pictures, words, dramatizations, and diagrams to represent answers, ideas, and procedures. When children can make connections among a variety of representations, their understanding of mathematical ideas is enhanced.

Becky believes that the best way for mathematics to be experienced and shared is through these five processes. Regardless of the specific mathematical topic, children should be actively engaged in solving problems, reasoning about what they encounter, communicating what they discover, building connections, and representing their ideas.

But what mathematical content, specifically, should be approached in this manner? Over her years of participating in professional development opportunities, working with colleagues, studying teacher resource materials, and jointly writing this book, Becky has organized kindergarten mathematics into six content strands that align well with NCTM's *Principles and Standards*:

1. Number and operation.
2. Patterns.
3. Sorting/comparing/ordering.
4. Geometry and spatial sense.
5. Measurement.
6. Data analysis/statistics/probability.

Number and *operation* activities need to pervade the kindergarten classroom. Children begin school with a variety of skills related to counting. The kindergarten classroom must build on these existing skills so that children develop additional counting strategies (counting on, for example); understand the concept of conservation of number; recognize relationships among numbers (four is one more than three, for example); and appreciate the many different uses of numbers in the real world. Early number-sense activities help build confidence with numbers and provide a foundation for later work with operations and estimation. Becky recognizes that her students need innumerable counting experiences, because counting is fundamental to mathematics.

Pattern explorations in kindergarten prompt children to look for relationships, find connections, and make predictions. Children should have many opportunities to create, describe, represent, compare, extend, and connect patterns. Patterns are the basis for understanding counting and numeration and help children develop basic reasoning strategies. Working with patterns also prompts children to make generalizations and lays the foundation for algebraic thinking. Some mathematicians refer to mathematics as the study of patterns. Becky's students dive right into this strand early in the year.

Sorting, comparing, and *ordering* are the processes that underlie geometry, measurement, number, and data analysis. Children discover properties of shapes by noting what is the same and what is different about them. Children often make comparisons as a way to interpret measurements and numerical data. They assign things an order according to attributes that they have been able to sort and compare. Children's natural curiosity leads them to sort, compare, and order, and Becky provides opportunities for her students to use these processes in their mathematical investigations throughout the year.

Geometry and spatial-sense explorations foster children's appreciation for both their physical world and the world of mathematics. Through spatial investigations children develop an intuitive feel for their environment. At this age, children need extensive experiences manipulating real objects so that they can begin to develop a tangible sense of the properties of two- and three- dimensional shapes. Students should also compare, match, draw, sort, and find shapes in the environment to support their emerging knowledge. Becky knows that it is easy to overlook geometry in kindergarten or to limit its study to the recognition of basic two-dimensional shapes, so she continues to search for ways to broaden this area of her curriculum.

Measurement is one of the most frequent uses of mathematics in daily life. Although young children are not ready to understand standard units of measure such as inches and centimeters, it is important to expose them to what it means to measure, to the various attributes of physical objects (length, width, height, weight, volume) that can be measured, and to the vocabulary associated with these attributes. They can also do some actual measuring using nonstandard units. Children's curiosity often provides the lead here as they ask such questions as *Does the green pail hold more sand than the pink one?* Becky emphasizes direct comparisons of objects and introduces the idea of using a third object to compare two other objects.

Data analysis, statistics, and *probability* investigations help children interpret information. Never before has our society been so dependent on communication and technology, and never before has the ability to understand and interpret data been so important. Becky believes children should be involved in open-ended investigations that require them to collect, organize, represent, and analyze data and make decisions and predictions based on that information. Such investigations foster an appreciation for the usefulness of mathematics and build self-confidence.

Big Ideas

While these general descriptions of the content strands are helpful to Becky, she delineates them further in order to better inform her teaching. Over the years, she has prepared a list of important ideas within the six content strands (see Figure 3.3). But just because major ideas for each strand are identified and listed separately does not mean that the ideas in one strand are not connected to those in others.

The items in Becky's list, which are all equally important, are the essential mathematical ideas she believes children wrestle with at this age. However, they are not goals for children to master by the end of kindergarten. Rather, a child's understanding of these big ideas will continue to grow, through repeated exposure and reflection. Furthermore, Becky's list continues to evolve as she learns more about mathematics and how children develop their mathematical understanding. Her students and her reflections about their work are her best resources for this continued evolvement.

Becky's knowledge of mathematics and her awareness of developmental patterns help her identify these ideas. The ideas then help her design workshop activities and link them into a series of coherent, related experiences—in other words, to build curriculum. The big ideas provide the focus, the purpose of the explorations. Knowing about developmental patterns helps her make connections and build bridges to future expected behavior. The clearer she is about the ideas she wants to develop and the manner in which they tend to unfold, the better able she is to develop a coherent curriculum for her students.

Number and Operation

- There are many different uses for number and many important numbers in our lives.
- Counting is a way to keep track of quantity.
- To count you need to associate one and only one number name with each object.
- There are different ways to count. How you count depends on the situation. For example, counting by twos makes sense when you are counting eyes.
- Sometimes you can estimate; an exact count is not always needed.
- You can join and take apart groups of objects. When you join them, you can find out how many there are altogether; when you take some away, you can find out how many are left. When you have two groups, you can see how many more one has than the other, or if the number in each group is the same.
- Numbers can be grouped with symbols.

Patterns

- Available information can help you predict what comes next.
- One type of pattern is a repeating pattern.
- Patterns can be found everywhere.
- Sometimes you need more information to make a generalization.
- Patterns can be represented symbolically.
- The same information can yield different patterns, depending on how you interpret the information.

Sorting/Comparing/Ordering

- Sorting, comparing, and ordering are ways to organize information.
- There are a variety of ways to sort, compare, and order.
- You may need to organize what you know in order to make comparisons.
- You can sort, compare, and order by more than one attribute.
- An object can simultaneously belong to more than one group.
- Specific terms are used for describing particular comparisons.

FIGURE 3.3 Mathematical ideas for the kindergarten classroom

Geometry and Spatial Sense

- Objects in our world can be described by their shape.
- Geometry helps us describe and organize the physical world.
- There are two-dimensional and three-dimensional shapes.
- Different shapes have different properties.
- Things look different when you see them from a different perspective.

Measurement

- Measurement is a tool for describing things in the world.
- Relational terms are relative; something may be either big or small, depending on the referents.
- You can compare objects directly or in relation to a third object.
- You can measure the attributes of length, weight, and capacity.
- A measurement must include a number and a unit.
- It may be more appropriate to use one unit rather than another unit to measure a particular object.

Data Analysis/Statistics/Probability

- You can use information to help you answer questions that interest you.
- Data must be collected. You need to figure out what you want to know and then find a good way to gather the information.
- How you organize and represent your data is important.
- Icons in a display can represent one unit or more than one unit.
- We use data to make predictions, connections, and draw conclusions.

FIGURE 3.3 Mathematical ideas for the kindergarten classroom (*continued*)

Planning for the Year

Over time, most teachers develop a sense of how the year should flow. In September Becky focuses on helping children understand what happens during math workshop and become familiar with the manipulatives used in the classroom. She establishes daily routines like the attendance stick and calendar activities. After a week of exploring manipulatives, the next week's activities are built around the children's names. Sorting, comparing, collecting data, and counting are all aspects of the initial activities in Becky's classroom. Through these activities, the children are exposed to a wide variety of mathematical content. They explore authentic data while learning about each other. They also learn how to work in groups and how to talk about mathematics.

It often takes most of September to establish general classroom expectations and a familiarity with the basic materials used in mathematics. Once this has been accomplished, Becky concentrates on mathematical investigations, pursuing a particular content strand. She usually starts with a unit on patterns, but sometimes she begins with a combined unit on geometry and measurement or one that deals with sorting/comparing/ordering in connection with data and chance. Becky then integrates these mathematically focused units into broader classroom themes such as harvest activities in the fall or the study of oceans in the spring.

Varying mathematical and interdisciplinary themes balances the curriculum and gives depth and breadth to the children's mathematical understanding. It is crucial that children experience mathematical ideas in ever deeper ways over a sustained period of time. However, they also need to experience the wide variety of arenas in which mathematical ideas can be investigated.

Thematic Units

Curriculum delivered through a textbook is usually organized within chapters. Nontextbook programs (which are more common in kindergarten), whether designed by the teacher or obtained commercially, are usually organized within units. A thematic unit may focus on an interdisciplinary topic, such as *neighborhoods*, or on a mathematical topic, such as *measurement*. Good sources of topics include existing curriculums, children's interests, special events, and literature.

Becky keeps her list of big ideas in mind as she plans thematic units. She wants to be sure she integrates mathematics in realistic and meaningful ways. She begins by brainstorming about the purpose of the unit, using questions to generate important ideas radiating from the central theme (see Figure 3.4).

This gives Becky a great start, but she now needs to concentrate on the mathematical connections. She reorders her web, again placing the theme in the center but this time using subject areas as the spokes, or arms. Under each subject she lists questions to address or activities to consider. (See Figure 3.5.)

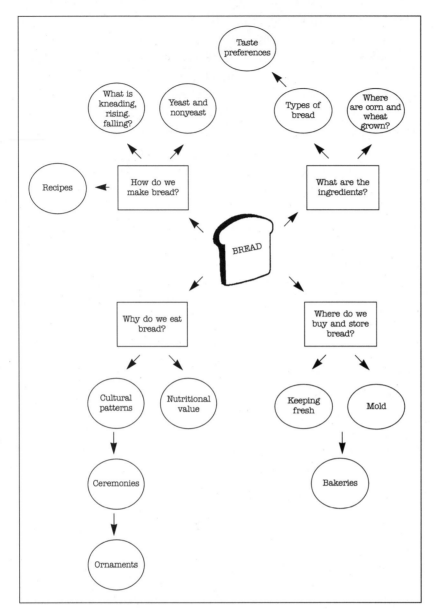

FIGURE 3.4 A thematic web around the topic *bread*

Becky notices that the mathematics she has identified looks somewhat meager. However, just creating an activity for math's sake doesn't make sense to her. Therefore, she searches for authentic mathematical experiences she can layer into the unit. The measurement needed to make bread is one very important one.

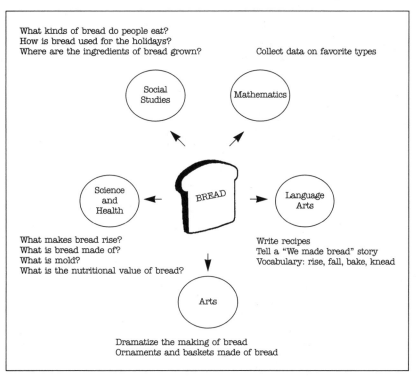

FIGURE 3.5 A subject-area web for the theme *bread*

She might also pose the following problem: I have 10 slices of bread; how many sandwiches can I make?

By combining webbing techniques like this, Becky has made sure she has identified connections among the disciplines *and* considered each content area adequately. Although teachers often use webs to develop interdisciplinary topics, not many use them to develop a mathematical content area, relying instead on commercial curriculum guides to identify the content to be "covered." While such resources are valuable, they are rarely organized to foster the development of ideas. By developing a web, or "content map," Becky is able to think more deeply about what the mathematics related to a thematic unit represents.

Becky creates her content map in stages. She begins with broad strokes and then focuses and refines it over time. Let's take another example, this time using Becky's big ideas related to investigations with data:

- Posing questions.
- Collecting data.
- Organizing and representing data.
- Analyzing and interpreting data.[2]

First, Becky thinks about questions associated with each process and comes up with an initial content map (see Figure 3.6).

Over time, she then thinks carefully about each of the four areas individually. For example, she brainstorms questions she might pose that would interest the children and perhaps serve as the focus of later investigations:

- How many letters are in our names?
- How many people are in our families?
- What do we like to do in the winter?
- What are our favorite cookies?

She makes sure that the list includes questions with categorical answers (e.g., colors, pets, types of food) as well as numerical answers and questions that may lead to messy data. For example, not all children will interpret a question about family size in the same way. If respondents are really answering different questions (*How many people live in your house?* or *How many people are in your extended family?*), their answers cannot be combined meaningfully, and they will need to decide what to do with such data or what new data to collect. Or again, data generated by the question *What is your favorite cookie?* is very different from that generated by *Do you like oatmeal or chocolate chip cookies better?* Too often, data investigations in kindergarten are oversimplified. The teacher forms the question in a way that identifies possible answers; decides how the data will be organized; and makes all the materials necessary to display the data. If that happens, only the teacher is doing any significant mathematical thinking! Becky has learned to consider who is really doing the work as she plans a thematic unit, a content unit, or her daily activities.

---

[2]In the upper elementary grades, Becky might separate the organization and representation of data or the analysis and interpretation of data, but combining them seems appropriate at this age.

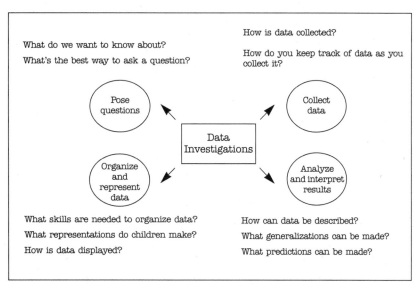

FIGURE 3.6   A content map of the mathematical processes associated with data investigations

Few teachers have time to do this type of analysis for all aspects of mathematics. However, we need to plan this way whenever we develop a new unit or think about refining a unit we're already using. Engaging in this reflective inquiry about our curriculum is a way to make sure that mathematical skills are nested within the development of mathematical ideas and that all important areas of the curriculum are represented adequately and authentically.

A Word About Support

Becky is grateful that she works in a system that encourages teachers to engage in such analysis at grade-level meetings. These meetings allow her to talk with other teachers whose students are the same age and developmental range, and who are subject to the same expectations and time limitations. These monthly meetings are an invaluable resource, an opportunity for teachers to discuss questions they have about their instructional plans and their students' learning. Within this rich support system, Becky is able to become the architect of her curriculum. Her understanding of the "big picture" informs the specific tasks she provides her students.

4

Choosing Mathematical Tasks

The mathematical tasks we select greatly influence what our students learn about mathematics and how they view it. If the tasks are fragmented, rote exercises unrelated to their questions, children learn that mathematics consists of memorizing unconnected rules that are unnecessary to their lives. If, however, the tasks emphasize the exploration of ideas, the creation of relationships, and the forming of conceptual understanding, mathematics becomes an exciting arena of sense making. Therefore, we need to think critically about the characteristics of worthwhile tasks.

When Is a Task Worthwhile?

Most of us recognize the worth of a particular mathematical task when we experience it with our students. The children are engaged, and the activity stimulates the communication of ideas and, when finished, leaves the children with something of mathematical value. Although it is more difficult to evaluate the merit of a task in the abstract, certain characteristics increase the likelihood that it will unfold in a worthwhile manner.

A Worthwhile Task Is Developmentally Appropriate
A teacher needs a general understanding of the developmental characteristics of children and the ways in which mathematical

ideas evolve in order to select and create worthwhile tasks. A mathematical task in kindergarten should:

- Focus on direct multisensory experiences and on activities that emphasize physical movement. Children need to be active, to use their senses and move their bodies.
- Focus on concrete experiences. Children need tactile stimulation and must be able to view concrete models. Using manipulatives is important.
- Encourage the natural development of oral language. Communication helps deepen understanding, and being able to use a common language allows children to communicate their ideas to one another and to their teacher.
- Encourage children to make observations and predictions. Such behavior allows children actively to construct knowledge that they will later be able to formalize.
- Prompt children to investigate ideas, albeit informally, related to conservation of number, length, area, weight, and volume. Tasks that involve counting and measuring should permeate the curriculum, but students should not be required to memorize basic facts nor to use standard measurement.
- Encourage children to represent mathematical ideas generated by their manipulation of physical objects. Although written symbols and words can be included in such representations, they should not be the focus of work at this level.

It is usually easy to tell when a task or concept is not developmentally appropriate: the children fidget, become distracted, or are easily frustrated. Sometimes a developmentally inappropriate idea will simply be ignored:

CHARLIE: [*Very tall for his age, looking across the room at Megan, who is petite*] Megan's a baby.

BECKY: WHY DO YOU SAY THAT?

CHARLIE: Because she's small.

BECKY: MEGAN'S THE SAME AGE AS YOU ARE, CHARLIE, AND I DON'T THINK SHE WOULD LIKE BEING CALLED A BABY.

CHARLIE: She's small, she's a baby.

BECKY: [*Knowing that she is shorter and older than Charlie's mother*] CHARLIE, YOUR MOM IS BIGGER THAN ME, BUT I AM OLDER THAN SHE IS.

CHARLIE: [*Struggling with this complex piece of information*] That doesn't matter—you're grown-ups, I'm a kid.

Charlie's level of development does not allow him to make sense of Becky's adult reasoning. Instead, he has found a way to dismiss her comment.

Knowing the basic ways in which mathematical ideas tend to unfold helps Becky create or select developmentally appropriate tasks. For example, Tali and Orin are playing a button game. Six buttons have been placed in each of two cups. Without looking, each child simultaneously takes a cup and removes some buttons from it. They record the number of buttons removed from each cup. Next, they take turns finding the total number of buttons removed, and each child records that number as well (see Figure 4.1).

When it is Tali's turn, she pushes her pile of buttons together with Orin's pile and counts them one by one as she moves them to the right. Orin has a different approach. He puts his hand over his buttons and says, "I have five." He then uses a counting-on strategy, counting each one of Tali's buttons, starting with six. Later, Becky asks several children to dramatize their counting

---

The Button Game

Name: Date:

Player #1   Player #2   Total # of Buttons

_____   _____   _____

_____   _____   _____

_____   _____   _____

FIGURE 4.1   A recording sheet for the Button Game

strategies. Conversations like this help children become more aware of their own techniques and expose them to the techniques of others.

Through experience and professional reading, Becky knows that the development of addition follows a similar course regardless of culture, race, gender, or class. Most prekindergarten children can combine a set of three and a set of two and, by counting each object, arrive at a total of five. Over time children learn the more efficient method of "counting on." Eventually, mental images replace the concrete objects. Much later, three plus two is automatically recognized as equivalent to five, and children can represent this relationship symbolically without needing to link it to a concrete model. Aware of this developmental path, Becky can choose tasks that build on children's informal uses of mathematical concepts and place each child's knowledge along that continuum.

The developmentally appropriate criterion is not meant to imply, however, that children should be able to proceed through tasks without difficulty. Such a learning environment would deny the importance of cognitive challenges in the stimulation of learning. Lev Vygotsky (1930), a Russian psychologist, introduced the notion of the "zone of proximal development": the distance between the child's actual and potential developmental levels. The actual level is determined by the problem solving the child can accomplish independently. The potential level is that which the child can accomplish with adult guidance or in collaboration with more capable peers. Worthwhile tasks awaken abilities and functions within the zone of proximal development and thus stimulate the developmental process.

The difference between what a child can accomplish alone and what that same child can do when working with others is amazing. First, listen as Becky and Mei talk about the number six:

BECKY: WHAT DO YOU KNOW ABOUT THE NUMBER SIX, MEI?

MEI: I know it's three plus three.

BECKY: DO YOU KNOW ANYTHING ELSE ABOUT THE NUMBER SIX?

MEI: No, it's just three plus three.

BECKY: [*Hoping to trigger other associations*] OKAY. CAN YOU COUNT TO SIX?

MEI: Yes, one, two, three, four, five, six.

BECKY: DOES THAT MAKE YOU THINK OF ANYTHING ELSE ABOUT SIX?

MEI: No.

Becky is curious about how the other children will respond to the question, so later at meeting time she asks the same question to the entire class.

BECKY: MEI AND I WERE HAVING A CONVERSATION THAT I WANT TO SHARE WITH YOU. I ASKED MEI WHAT SHE KNEW ABOUT THE NUMBER SIX. WHAT DO YOU KNOW ABOUT THE NUMBER SIX?

HALEY: I'm six.

MEI: Three plus three is six.

BEN: Seven comes next.

JOSÉ: My house is number six.

KIMI: There's a six on the clock.

ROSITA: One more than five is six.

MEI: There are six people in my family.

Alone, Mei is able to think of only one idea about six. As a member of a group, she is able to share in a conversation in which several uses of number and other arithmetic facts about six are identified. She is able to broaden her thinking and provide a new example.

A Worthwhile Task Focuses on Significant Mathematics

A worthwhile task should encourage children to gain insights into the structure of mathematics and the relationships within mathematics. It should also cultivate the discovery of strategies for pursuing and representing mathematical ideas. The same task may or may not address important mathematical ideas and strategies, depending on how and when it is addressed.

Becky used to have her students cut out pictures of shapes from magazines. Her intention was to help children relate geometry to the real world. After she began to think more critically about the mathematics embedded in such tasks, she no longer found this activity worthwhile. First, most of the children's time is devoted to cutting, a physical task that requires a rather intense concentration on fine motor skills, rather than to mathematical thinking. Further, the mathematics is somewhat troubling. Children basically locate objects that they already think are a particular shape. For example, they find a picture of a pizza as an example of a circle and then cut it out. Not only does this do little to further understanding of geometry, it might even provide the false notion that a circle is a three-dimensional shape. The pizza, while represented by a circle on a two-dimensional page, is really more like a very short cylinder.

Even at the kindergarten level, exploration of geometric shapes in the real world can be more mathematically focused. Becky now asks children to respond to what-if questions like *What would happen if a kickball were shaped like a cube?* After they talk about it for a while, she has the students test the difference between kicking a sphere and kicking a cube.

The significance of mathematics is also increased when the generalization *math is everywhere* is addressed explicitly. Becky encourages her students to look for shapes outdoors at recess, within their classroom, and at home. She pairs these activities with what-if questions that help children identify the properties of specific shapes and relate those properties to the functions of the real-world objects. Without the broader arena and the probing questions, the mathematics is incidental and not too different from a workbook page that requires children to mark an X on each circle.

A Worthwhile Task Is Contextualized

Situated learning puts a task within an authentic context that is meaningful to children. Such authenticity is one way to capture students' interest and establish a task's value. It may even give children insights on how to begin. Consider the decontextualized question *What is one less than nine?* This question is difficult because it requires children to reverse the order of numbers. Without a context to motivate their thinking, the task is arbitrary. Why should children want to pursue a task that is both difficult and arbitrary?

However, children listening to the story *Ten in a Bed* (Dale 1988) are motivated to predict the number of animals left in bed after one falls out. Using ten teddy bear counters, children can dramatize the story as they listen. The meaning of *one less than* becomes clear. They can count their bears in order to predict the new number of animals left in the bed. Within this context, the task achieves an appropriate level of difficulty. After exploring the animals-rolling-out-of-bed problem, children might explore a problem about birds flying off a branch. Only when they have worked with a variety of contextualized settings and have a firm grasp of how to model and represent these situations should de-contextualized questions be added to the mix.

Sometimes Becky identifies settings by listening to her students' explorations. In early spring she overhears this conversation:

KAITLIN: Hey, let's play dress-up. I want the black hat.

LISA: I want to wear the green shoes.

TANYA: Okay. I'll wear the black high heels.

CHARLIE: I'm going to use all of these bracelets. [*He puts eleven plastic bracelets on his arm.*]

LISA: That's not fair!

CHARLIE: Uh-huh.

KAITLIN: How about if we share the bracelets? If everyone gets one, then it will be fair. [*After protesting a bit more, Charlie gives each of the three girls one bracelet. He leaves the others on his arm, which he shakes widely to make the bangles jingle.*]

LISA: That's still not fair. You have more that you can share.

CHARLIE: Oh, all right. [*He gives one more bracelet to each of the girls, leaving him with five.*]

LISA: We can have one more each.

CHARLIE: No way!

KAITLIN: That's right. Then Charlie would only have two bracelets.

CHARLIE: Yeah, and you have shoes anyway.

Within the natural context of playing dress-up, the children have explored ideas related to sharing, one of the meanings of division. They have also grappled with what fair means in this situation. At the meeting after recess, Becky asks Kaitlin, Lisa, Tanya, and Charlie to tell how they shared the bracelets.

CHARLIE: They were all mine, but then I shared.

LISA: Charlie gave us each some bracelets.

CHARLIE: I still had more.

KAITLIN: That was fair. We had other stuff.

BECKY: IMAGINE THAT THERE WERE TWO GIRLS AND A BOY PLAYING DRESS-UP. HOW COULD THEY SHARE TEN BRACELETS?

TREVOR: They could each get some.

ANA: Like maybe two.

KIMI: Or the girls could keep them.

KAITLIN: That's not fair.

BECKY: IN MATH WORKSHOP TODAY I WANT YOU TO DECIDE HOW MANY BRACELETS EACH CHILD GETS.

Becky has the children retell the story problem several times. Then, they all scurry off to pursue the task in small groups. (Becky has borrowed bracelets from the other kindergarten classes so that three groups of children can work directly with real materials. An idea-centered curriculum often requires additional materials. Having colleagues who are willing to share is extremely helpful.)

Haley's group, which doesn't have real bracelets, uses the two-color counters, "because they are round." Haley takes ten counters and places three of them on the table, separate from one another. Then she adds another counter to each of the single counters, making three groups of two. She looks at the four counters left, counts them, and pauses. She then puts another counter in each group and moves the remaining counter far away from the three groups of counters. Next, she organizes the grouped counters into a three-by-three array. Becky learns from Haley's recorded work that the tenth bracelet is for Haley's mom. (See Figure 4.2.)

Children are quite familiar with sharing. The leftover bracelet in this problem appears to be more of a social than a mathematical problem for these students. They have strong feelings about sharing fairly and most ignore the tenth bracelet or, like Haley, find a way to separate it from the three children. Some children make three groups of three and then give the "extra" to one of the children in the story. In their playful way, they identify with this child and enjoy telling everyone, "I got the most bracelets." Since the children have not been exposed to a series of

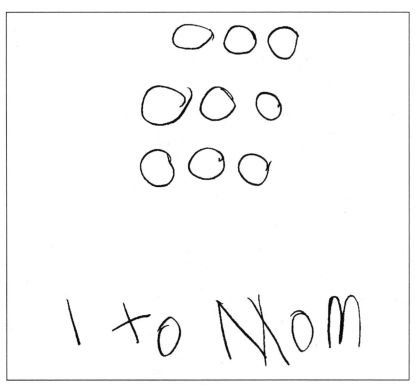

FIGURE 4.2 Haley's drawing showing her division of ten bracelets

contrived division problems that all come out evenly, they are not perplexed by a remainder. The mathematics makes sense to them in this setting.

A Worthwhile Task Offers an Appropriate Challenge

Worthwhile tasks are geared to an appropriate level of difficulty. Tasks should not be presented in bite-size chunks that eliminate all procedural decisions and cognitive challenge. On the other hand, they should not be so broad that they overwhelm the children and leave them not knowing where to begin. Just as the question *How many chins do you have?* is too simple, the query *How many chins are there in this school today?* is too difficult. An important part of the art of teaching is to decide how to provide an appropriate balance of support and provocation. Becky must challenge children in order to instigate the growth of ideas, but that challenge must lie within the children's reach. As Kathy

Richardson has said, "[The] goal is to give all of the children in a classroom activities that keep them thinking and working at the edge of their understanding" (1997, p. 432).

Sometimes this balance is reached by adjusting the numbers used in a problem. In the bracelet problem, the number of children and number of bracelets could be altered in order to make the problem more or less challenging. While the size of the numbers is not as important as what the children are asked to do with those numbers, it does influence problem difficulty. Becky thinks about both number size and the operations a task requires as she considers what is appropriate for her students.

A few days after the children explored the bracelet problem, Becky poses a new problem:

> 2 children are having a snack.
> They have 5 cookies to share.
> How many cookies does each child get?

Again, children work in groups and use a variety of materials to aid their thinking. Some children are insistent that each child gets two cookies and that the remaining cookie be given to Becky or even thrown away. To them, sharing means that everyone gets exactly the same amount, no more, no less. Others feel just as strongly that the leftover cookie should be distributed. Mei says, "Some people like cookies more than others. Maybe they should get the last one." A few even suggest breaking a cookie in half. When this idea is introduced at a whole-class meeting, some children are persuaded that this is the best solution. Jamal says, "Why didn't I think of that?" Other children hold to their original thinking. Seth explains, "I don't think so. It's hard to break a cookie in half. You don't get very much."

Becky was intrigued by the differences in mathematical thinking generated by the bracelet and cookie problems. New options were available with cookies, since, unlike bracelets, they can be broken in half. The number of cookies, five, and the number of children, two, were fewer than the numbers in the bracelet problem. The type of thinking, however, was more sophisticated. For Becky, these problems illustrate the complexity of analyzing task difficulty.

A Worthwhile Task Allows for Multiple Perspectives

Tasks that encourage multiple perspectives make it easier to meet the needs of a variety of learners. Such tasks are sometimes referred to as *open ended*. Tasks can be open in different ways. For instance, they may encourage:

- Various interpretations.
- Various methods of exploration.
- Various materials.
- Various responses.
- Various representations.
- Various related mathematical ideas.

Tasks that encompass multiple perspectives are richer than those that do not. They allow for a greater number of choices to be made and learning needs to be met. They generate interest in communication, because children are eager to share ideas that are different from someone else's. Most important, such tasks empower learners to follow their own mathematical hunches and instincts. Following their own hunches allows children to experience their powerful roles as learners of mathematics.

One way Becky tries to encourage multiple perspectives is to provide learners with a wide range of materials. For example, if children are exploring problems about people getting in and out of a boat, she cuts a large piece of oil cloth into the shape of a boat. Some of the children stand on and off the cloth to dramatize the actions in the problems. For others, she provides Velcro-backed felt people and a felt boat. Some children are able to work with teddy bear counters, and still others are able to model the problems with tiles or drawings. Each child is able to pursue the activity with the correct level of supportive materials.

How Can I Create a Worthwhile Task?

The prospect of creating or selecting tasks that are developmentally appropriate, focus on significant mathematics, have a real-world context, offer appropriate challenges, and encourage multiple perspectives is daunting! In some tasks, some of these characteristics are more dominant than others. Some tasks are more appealing to some children than to others. What is most important is that over time, by working through a variety of tasks, every child will engage in worthwhile mathematical work.

Relate a Task to a Classroom Event

One way to develop tasks is to relate them to classroom events and issues. During the first few days of school, Becky introduces the children to a literacy activity (which she learned from her friend Bobbi Fisher) that focuses on children's names. The children, with Becky's help, learn to "read" (in unison) the nursery rhyme "Jack Be Nimble," which is displayed on the literacy easel for all to see. One at a time, each of the children's names is used in place of *Jack*. Each time the class rereads the rhyme using the child's name as Becky points to the words. While the rhyme is chanted, that child jumps over a candlestick.

Becky connects this literacy activity to a series of mathematical tasks she has created. Following this shared reading, most of the children engage in their own explorations while Becky holds a small-group math workshop with six children. She asks these children to get a work can and join her at a nearby table, on which she has placed a bucket of Unifix cubes.

Becky begins the small-group workshop with a question: "How many letters are there in your name?" The children work independently trying to answer the question. Children with names of three or four letters respond quickly. Most children with longer names find it more difficult.

ALLISON: Each time I try to count my letters I keep thinking I already had them.

BECKY: WHAT COULD YOU DO ABOUT THAT?

ALLISON: Can I write my name down?

BECKY: OF COURSE, IF YOU THINK IT WOULD HELP.

ALLISON: Oh boy, would it.

As the children determine the number of letters in their name, Becky asks them to snap together that many Unifix cubes. Then the children tell Becky the number of letters in their name and Becky hands them a strip containing that many dot stickers. Mario, for example, receives a row of five stickers:

The children then write the letters in their name on the dots and stick them, in order, to their train of cubes, one to a cube. As the children work Becky notes how they determine the number of letters, how they count out the number of cubes and dots to take, whether or not they ever double-check their counts, and any counting errors they may make. She also makes sure that names are spelled correctly, helping if needed.

When everyone has finished, the trains are laid in the center of the table:

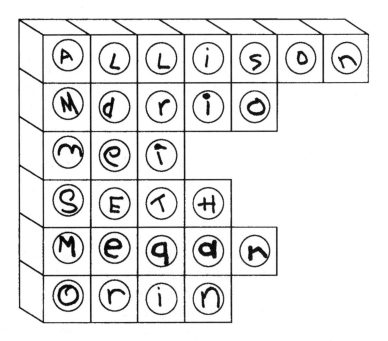

BECKY: WHOSE NAME BEGINS WITH THE LETTER M?

MEGAN: Mine does.

MEI: Mine does.

MARIO: Mine does, too!

BECKY: HOW MANY NAMES IS THAT?

SETH: Three.

BECKY: HOW DO YOU KNOW?

SETH: I counted the names.

MEGAN: You could count the people.

BECKY: WHOSE NAMES ARE FOUR LETTERS LONG?

ORIN: Mine is and Seth's is, too.

BECKY: CAN YOU FIND A NAME WITH EXACTLY SIX LETTERS? [*The children count each row of cubes several times, determining the number of letters in each name.*]

MEI: I don't see any.

ALLISON: That's a tricky question.

BECKY: WHOSE NAME HAS THE GREATEST NUMBER OF LETTERS?

ALLISON: That's me.

BECKY: HOW DID YOU DECIDE?

ALLISON: It's the longest.

BECKY: IS THERE ANOTHER WAY TO TELL?

ORIN: You can count.

Pursuing this activity early in the year allows Becky to engage children in meaningful investigations right away. It also gives her the opportunity to observe her students at work. She makes quick notes about the ways the children count, their name and letter recognition skills, and how they work in a teacher-directed group. (Her students' abilities to listen to, interpret, and follow through on directions are on Becky's mind a lot during the first days of school, because these skills are so pivotal to success in the classroom.)

Follow-up activities throughout the rest of the week include sorting the class "name trains" by first letter, locating individual letters in a name on an alphabet chart, and ordering names by the number of letters. These "name" activities are linked mathematically because they involve data collection, organization, representation, and interpretation. Through these activities Becky is able to expose the children to a variety of mathematical ideas early in the year. Such exposure broadens students' perceptions of what mathematics is. (For a complete description of this activity see Murray et al. 1998).

Build a Task on Children's Questions

Another way to create worthwhile tasks is to build them around children's questions. Children naturally ask questions as they encounter their world, and their questions are by definition authentic. By creating tasks in response to these questions, teachers are taking advantage of teachable moments. However, while these moments are easily recognized, what to do about them may not be.

Simple questions, ones that merely embellish an activity or are answered quickly, are easily integrated into the task at hand. Questions that arise between activities may be resolved on the spot with a brief miniactivity. Questions asked by an individual child or a small group of children during an exploration can be addressed with that child or group without disrupting the learning path of others.

Let's look at an example of the latter. Nicole has surveyed her classmates to find out how many have a sister. Discovering that fifteen of her classmates have a sister, she wants to record the symbol for that number. She asks Becky, "How do you write fifteen?" Becky decides that Nicole has forgotten how to write the numeral rather than that she is unable to make one of the digits. Therefore she asks Nicole where she might find the number fifteen written in the classroom. When Nicole says, "I'm not sure," Ezra, a student working nearby, suggests the calendar. Together, Ezra and Nicole go to the calendar to look for the number. By being encouraged to find the number rather than being told, "You write a one and then a five," Nicole learns how to get the information herself. She can follow the same procedure if a similar question arises later.

In this example, Nicole's question needed to be answered in order for her to complete her task, only two children were involved, and very little time was required. It was obvious that the question should be addressed and that it was easy to do so right then. Unfortunately, it is not always so clear what to do. For example:

- When the child's question is not directly related to completing the current activity successfully, should that activity stop in order to pursue the question?
- When one child asks a question during a whole-class meeting or discussion, should the entire group focus on that question right then?

- When a question requires a considerable amount of investigation, should time be devoted to the question immediately?

Sometimes a question or an event is so pivotal that activity must stop and it must be addressed. For example, one day Becky is reading the nursery rhyme "Itsy Bitsy Spider" when a spider, attached to its woven web, dangles right in front of her eyes. This unexpected coincidence is too unusual to ignore. Becky puts aside her intended focus, which was nursery rhymes, and brings out a number of books about spiders.

As part of their investigation, the children learn that spiders have eight legs. Becky shifts the day's math task to finding out how many legs there are if there are two spiders. Kaitlin draws a picture of two spider bodies. Then she draws eight legs on each body. She counts to find sixteen and talks about "two groups of eight legs." Although she does not record the total, she says, "Here are my two spiders with sixteen legs," when she shows her drawing (see Figure 4.3) at meeting time.

Sometimes circumstances do not require or allow unexpected events or children's questions to be pursued immediately. One day, Becky is ready to introduce a social/emotional activity in which the children will sit on chairs in a circle (this distinguishes the activity from a class meeting, when they sit on the rug). The children have gathered on the rug, and Becky tells them they must each get a chair. Tanya responds, "Do you think we have enough chairs for everyone to sit?"

Becky needs to make a choice. At first she finds the question

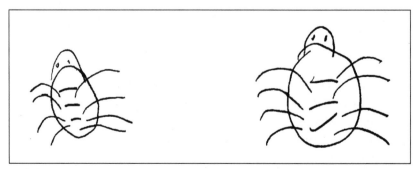

FIGURE 4.3 Kaitlin's drawing of two spiders with sixteen legs

somewhat odd. All the children sit in chairs at the same time while they are eating their snacks. Then she realizes that the chairs are spread all over the room then; perhaps Tanya doesn't understand that the number of chairs will be the same once they are brought into the meeting area. She recognizes the mathematical significance of the question but also knows that Tanya's query will be trivial once the children each get a chair. Besides, she has already set the stage for something else. Addressing this question is not necessary for the planned activity to proceed. Nevertheless, Becky doesn't want to give the impression that Tanya's question doesn't matter or to lose this opportunity for authentic mathematics. Therefore she tells the children, "Tanya's question makes me wonder how many chairs we have in our classroom. We will come back to this question later."

The next day's math workshop begins this way:

BECKY: YESTERDAY TANYA WONDERED IF WE HAD ENOUGH CHAIRS FOR OUR MEETING. DID WE? [*Everyone nods.*] THAT QUESTION MADE ME THINK OF ANOTHER ONE. [*Becky reads what she has written on the mathematics easel.*] "HOW MANY CHAIRS ARE THERE IN OUR CLASSROOM?" [*She turns to the children.*] HOW DO YOU THINK WE COULD FIND OUT?

LISA: We could all go sit in a chair.

BEN: We can bring all of the chairs onto the rug and count them.

ROSITA: Then there won't be enough room for us!

The children decide they will go and count the chairs. There is a certain amount of disarray: "I can't remember what comes after nineteen." "I can't remember if I already counted this one." The children return to the rug with a variety of answers and some noticeable levels of frustration.

"What made this so difficult?" Becky asks. The children agree that it is too hard to keep track of which chairs have been counted. After some more discussion, someone suggests putting one cube on each chair and then collecting the cubes and counting them.

At this point, Becky could have led the children around the room, directing a child to place a cube on a chair while the class said the number aloud. Such an approach, however, is too dependent on teacher leadership. Instead, Becky gives each child a cube and tells him or her to place it on a chair. After everyone has done so, it is clear that there are enough chairs for each child to sit in one at the same time. But the children also notice that there are more chairs to count. They look for chairs without cubes and place cubes on them as well. The children then collect the cubes and make a long train. Together, they count the cubes and answer the question. Once they agree that there are thirty-four chairs in the room, Becky asks, "How many chairs would there be if we moved them all to the meeting area?" Tanya responds, "The same, thirty-four." (Tanya's response does not mean that she can now conserve number, but Becky is pleased by the sureness of her response.)

Tanya's original question (*Do we have enough chairs for everyone to sit?*) did not warrant a whole-class investigation. As a result, it was broadened. No one, including Becky, knew exactly how many chairs there were in the classroom.

Classroom events and children's questions can lead to wonderful teachable moments. If only such moments happened daily in some predictable fashion! While Becky can get better at listening to her students and capitalizing on their questions, at viewing unpredictable events as inspirational rather than interruptive, and at weaving significant mathematics into unexpected places, such opportunities are not frequent enough or sequential enough to provide a well-developed and balanced curriculum.

Adapt an Existing Task

In Becky's experience, an existing task that she discovers or rediscovers can stimulate her thinking. The task, however, usually needs to be adapted, perhaps to make it more open or to give it a more appropriate level of difficulty or to present it within a more appropriate context.

Even the simplest exercises can be redesigned into appropriate tasks. Consider all those workbook pages in which students are asked to count the number of objects and circle the numeral that represents that quantity. The activity is not situated, cannot be revisited, and stimulates little or no curiosity. Now consider that same activity within a week that focuses on the fall harvest in general and on apples in particular. Students have tasted, touched, smelled, and looked closely at different types of apples and engaged in other apple-focused activities.

During this week, Becky works with the children in small groups. Each child is given a felt tree with a number from one through six on it and asked to place that number of felt apples on the tree. The children spontaneously compare their trees and place them in order, by number. Then they exchange "trees" and repeat the activity. The "trees" and "apples" are also available to work on during explorations. Then the children are given a sheet with pictures of trees on which they draw apples and record how many apples they draw. The children can choose any numbers they wish (Megan includes three numbers greater than six—see Figure 4.4).

FIGURE 4.4 Megan's drawing of apples on a tree

Although the basic activity is similar to that found in workbooks, it has been transformed. Objects are manipulated, the activity can be revisited, the children can choose the numbers they use, and the context is meaningful.

Not all tasks need so much revision. Sometimes a change of context is the only thing needed to make a task more meaningful to students. Appropriate contexts can be:

- Suggested by the mathematics involved (setting up a class post office as a way to explore the sizes and shapes of boxes and envelopes, for example).
- Integrated with a thematic unit (making graphs of how children travel to school during a transportation unit, for example).
- Linked to children's natural activities (exploring one-to-one correspondence while setting the table when playing house, for example).
- Taken from a favorite picture book or story.

Also, many tasks can be explored over and over again. Minor changes allow children to explore the same tasks several days in a row (the pattern activities described in Chapter 1, for example). Some tasks (the attendance activities described in Chapter 2, for example) can be explored every day without any changes, as part of the classroom's daily routine.

Becky has identified four types of number problems that she can use many times with only modest alterations (the nouns and numbers in these examples can be changed to make "new" problems).

1. How many heads are there in this room?
2. I have seven pets. Some are gerbils and some are goldfish. How many of each type of pet do I have?[1]
3. I have six stones in all. Four stones are in my hand and the rest are in my pocket. How many stones are in my pocket?
4. I see four tulips. Each tulip has five petals. How many petals do I see in all?

---

[1]Chapter 9 focuses exclusively on this type of problem and how revisiting a problem like this fosters the development of mathematical ideas over time.

Where Does Professional Development Fit In?

It is impossible to overemphasize how important it is for teachers to understand mathematics themselves and to think about how children reach their mathematical understanding. Becky's intense interest in the field of elementary school mathematics and her continuous involvement in professional development projects has dramatically influenced her thinking about teaching and learning. She has come to recognize that as a kindergarten teacher she has sometimes overlooked or oversimplified the complex mathematics that her students can do.

The mathematics of kindergarten is often difficult for adults to appreciate, since skills such as counting are so easy from an adult perspective. By learning more adult mathematics, Becky has regained an appreciation for how hard one must work to learn new ideas. Consequently, she has thought more about the tasks she offers her students, the climate she creates for learning, and how the use of language plays a constant role in the growth of mathematical ideas.

5

Learning to Talk and Listen

What instructional patterns were followed when most of us were elementary school students? Did our teachers encourage us to express our ideas, ask questions, make presentations, debate opinions, and listen carefully to other students doing the same? For most of us, when these activities did occur, they did so only during language arts and social studies. But *no talking* was the clear message of mathematics instruction. In a perverse way, such a message made sense, because there were only two types of classroom activities in mathematics.

First, we watched the teacher compute in order to learn the one correct way to find answers to similar exercises. Asking questions then was to be avoided at all costs, because it announced to everyone that we were incapable of understanding the teacher. We spoke in response to a teacher's pauses, which occurred at the end of statements such as *A three-sided figure is called a . . .* or to questions such as *Linda, what is seven plus eight minus two?* It was a worksheet given orally; the pauses and question marks were the blanks.

The other and more predominant activity was "seat work," which focused exclusively on arithmetic. There was no peer teaching during such work, no alternative methods were allowed, and checking an answer with a classmate was considered cheating.

Thus, if we were talking, we were cheating or talking about something other than mathematics, both forbidden activities. So the rule became *no talking*.

Obviously Becky does not want to re-create such a classroom. To support the growth of ideas, she wants children to talk and listen to one another, to build on one another's insights, to negotiate common understanding, and to share invented strategies. She wants mathematics to be a social activity and her classroom to be a place where mathematical inquiry is cultivated. Participating in mathematical conversations is central to such inquiry. As Rebecca Corwin says,

> Students use language to present their ideas to each other, build theories together, share solution strategies, and generate definitions. Children's conversation is playful, urgent, and mathematical—they exchange observations, clarify their own and others' ideas, agree, disagree, and challenge one another. By talking—to themselves and to others—students form, speak, test, and revise ideas. (1996, p. 7)

Even if allowed, such behavior would not have occurred when many of us were in elementary school. The tasks themselves did not warrant such reactions. There were no theories to build and no ideas to revise; they were all provided by the teacher. Good tasks that illicit the desire to speak, listen, and share ideas are essential to promoting mathematical conversations. Good tasks alone, however, are not sufficient.

Math talk is risky for many teachers and students, perhaps because it is so unfamiliar. It requires students to share ideas that are not yet completely formed and to challenge the thinking of others. It requires teachers to follow up on what children are saying, to let children's desire to make sense of things direct their activities. In order to encourage her students to participate in this risky behavior, Becky must create a classroom atmosphere of mutual trust and respect.

Kindergarten teachers tend to be particularly aware of children's need for a favorable atmosphere like this. After all, just coming to kindergarten is initially a risk for most young children. It is possible, however, to provide a supportive environment for children without developing their trust and respect for mathematical conversations. In Becky's classroom, this trust and respect is built from mathematical experiences that allow each student to conclude that Becky and the other children:

- Are interested in what he or she thinks.
- Listen carefully to what she or he says.
- Assume he or she is doing and saying what makes sense to him or her.
- Will follow up on her or his ideas.

Children are more likely to draw such conclusions in classrooms where math talk is prevalent. When ways to address tasks are neither unique nor immediately obvious, children want to talk about their ideas. Asking probing questions also stimulates talk. Given time to formulate their thoughts, children often respond with a variety of ideas that can trigger further conversations. Since such talk is meaningful, both the teacher and the children listen attentively; they are interested in others' responses.

Talking While Working

Children tend to be egocentric by nature, and parallel play is common. It takes time to develop a sense of community. Early in the year it is not unusual to hear, *Hey, that was my idea. You can't copy it.* Over time, however, most children become more interested in working together and sharing their ideas. Later in the year, a child may say, *You built it like mine. Let's put it together and see how big it is.* Opportunities for mathematical conversations increase when children investigate mathematical ideas in pairs or in small groups. Children are likely to make comments and ask questions like these:

- Why are you doing that?
- I think I will line up my bears in twos, like you did.
- Let's see how long we can make it.
- Do you think this will come out like the other one?
- This is just like yours.

Such comments and questions arise naturally. They provide a way for children to respond to the activity at hand. The children are making predictions, plans, and comparisons. Most important, they are demonstrating their interest in sharing their thinking and their products.

Once students need and want to work together, as opposed to next to each other, communication follows. When tasks are defined jointly, conflicts and problems are bound to arise. Teachers often think of such interplay in terms of social interaction and conflict resolution, but these moments can also lead to powerful mathematical investigations.

Let's look at an example. Five of Becky's students are constructing a "castle" out of unit blocks. They carefully alternate unit and double-unit blocks in the individual walls they build and are delighted to find that the alternating pattern is maintained when they connect their structures to form their rectangular castle. They declare that their pattern "works perfectly." Then they negotiate their next step.

JAMAL: I know, let's make a floor.

MEGAN: Let's use the pattern blocks. [*They bring the tub of pattern blocks over to their structure and begin randomly placing blocks inside.*]

SETH: No, let's just use the yellow ones.

KIMI: I like those. They look like a beehive. [*The children begin to match the edges of the yellow hexagons[1] to create a "tile" floor for their castle. Some of the pieces meet the edge of the unit blocks, but some do not.*]

SAMMY: Why won't they all fit?

JAMAL: Some of them fit.

SAMMY: I know but I want them all to.

MEGAN: [*Finding that one of the red trapezoids fits in the opening created by the edges of the yellow hexagons and the unit-block walls*] We can put red here.

SAMMY: No . . . I want it all to be yellow.

---

[1] Although pattern blocks are three-dimensional, they are known by the shape of their top face.

JAMAL:	Let's keep trying. [*The children attempt to add more yellow hexagon pieces to their tile floor; they try moving the unit blocks back; they take some of the already-placed yellow hexagons out and reposition them. No matter what they do, they cannot make a floor that is all yellow and that is even with the walls of the castle. Though highly engaged, they are getting frustrated.*]
MEGAN:	I like it with red and yellow.
SAMMY:	No.
SETH:	Let's go ask Miss Eston. [*They go barreling over to Becky.*]
SAMMY:	We have a problem.
BECKY:	WHAT IS IT?
JAMAL:	We made a castle and we want to use the yellow hexagons to make a floor. It won't work.
BECKY:	WHAT DO YOU MEAN, IT WON'T WORK?

When the children bring Becky over to look at the castle, she realizes that what they are calling their "problem" is an interesting challenge in geometric design. Although hexagons *tessellate* (cover a flat surface without leaving any space uncovered), they cannot exactly fill a rectangular shape. When hexagon tiles are used as floor covering, the tiles around the edges of the room are cut to meet the walls. Becky wonders how to help the children recognize the complexity of their dilemma without snuffing their excitement. Because they are already frustrated, she decides to suggest the impossibility of their goal.

BECKY:	DO YOU THINK IT WILL EVER WORK?
MEGAN:	Yes, if we use the red ones.
SAMMY:	No, I don't want to use the reds.
SETH:	I think it will work if we build the castle over.
JAMAL:	I don't think it will ever work.
KIMI:	I don't know. It looks so pretty, though.

Becky encourages the children to build a little longer and heads back to work with other children. After a short while she returns to the block area. Kimi and Jamal have moved on to other things. Seth, Megan, and Sammy are still repositioning blocks.

BECKY:	WHAT DID YOU FIND OUT?
SAMMY:	Nothing.
SETH:	We're still trying.
MEGAN:	I still think we need to use red.

The castle remains standing in the block area for several days, its floor unfinished. Then one day Becky notices that red trapezoids have been carefully placed on two sides of the castle to form a straight edge with the unit blocks. The spaces on the other two sides are still there.

BECKY:	WHAT'S HAPPENING IN THE CASTLE?
MEGAN:	I put in some red ones.
SAMMY:	Yeah.
SETH:	We decided to use everyone's ideas.

In many ways the interaction among these children is unique. They are able to communicate with each other in mature ways. Is this really possible for children in kindergarten? It is, of course, but since teachers are needed by so many children, they often miss opportunities to observe their students tackling such authentic problems and having such wonderful conversations.

Becky could easily have overlooked this important piece of work. The reality of every classroom is that a teacher's attention is in high demand. Though the unit blocks are a vital material in her classroom, Becky has found that when students engage in unit-block construction, the work becomes the children's domain, not hers. Since they are so independent at building and so free with their ideas for play, she seldom, if ever, plays a key role in the block area. As a result, it is important for her to remember to take the time to listen to conversations that develop during this type of activity. In addition, students must trust that she is available to them and interested in their constructions. Her willingness to address their needs helps the children stay invested in their work.

Becky found the tenacity these children exhibited while working together on the castle exciting. They could easily have dismissed the challenge they stumbled on while playing with the unit blocks. Some children, whether working alone or in a group, move quickly to new ideas rather than wrestle with a problem as complex as tiling a floor. Developing tenacity in relation to a task is important. By sharing ideas and articulating where they were stuck, the children were able to stay focused. Yes, Kimi and Jamal moved on to other work after a while, but the other three children continued to work on the challenge until they finally agreed on a solution.

Although working in pairs or groups encourages conversations, children may also talk out loud when alone. For example, one day Ben is counting bears and drawing a picture to represent the number of bears counted. He is working independently, somewhat separated from any other children. After making his drawing he says, "Now let me check. If I put one bear on top of each picture, I'll know I'm right." Becky is pleased when she hears Ben talking to himself, because it is an important part of his work. Verbalizations like this help children stay focused, keep track of what they are doing, and clarify their thinking.

Children should be immersed in the sounds of mathematical language. They should practice "thinking out loud," explaining their ideas, and talking about what they have learned. Sometimes Becky needs to encourage individual children to describe their thinking. Prompts like *Tell me what you are doing* can stimulate the articulation of reasoning and problem-solving processes. These processes involve relationships between and among ideas, and children therefore use words like *because, if, then, sometimes, all, some,* and *none*. In addition, reasoning and problem solving often also involve prediction, reflection, and generalization, and children therefore use phrases like *I might, I wonder if,* and *I think* as well. Finally, many children use ordinal numbers when they enumerate their "thinking steps" in solving a problem.

Here's an example. José is working with a balance scale. There is a large rock on one pan of the scale and many small stones on the other pan.

BECKY: CAN YOU TELL ME WHAT YOU ARE DOING?

JOSÉ: I want to make the sides the same.

BECKY: HOW CAN YOU DO THAT?

JOSÉ: [*Pointing to the side that contains the small stones and is lower*] I think I keep adding here.

BECKY: WHY DO YOU THINK THAT?

JOSÉ: 'Cause when I take them away it's more different. I tried that first. [*Continuing to add stones as they talk*] Hey, I got it.

BECKY: WHAT DOES THIS TELL YOU?

JOSÉ: If I keep adding, then I can make it the same. These stones are the same as this rock.

José does not use the word *balance, weight,* or *unit,* but he is building ideas of equivalence and comparison. He can identify his actions and explain why he is taking them. He can make a summary statement about his work. Talking about his thinking helps him solidify his ideas and make the experience more meaningful.

For Becky, listening to children talk while they work is a privilege; she learns so much from them. She becomes familiar with their natural language for mathematical ideas, gains insights into their intuitive understanding and budding strategies, and gathers evidence of learning that informs her plans. Questions Becky thinks about as she reflects on the math talk in her classroom include:

- What activities this week stimulated the most talk about mathematics?
- Can I categorize the statements children make during this mathematical investigation?
- How do the types of mathematical comments a particular child makes vary from day to day?
- How does my joining a group affect children's mathematical conversations?
- How do the children monitor their own conversations?

Teachers as Listeners

Listening is not a passive activity; it is a complex action requiring the listener to process incoming data in order to make meaning (Jalango 1995). Unfortunately, most teacher education is aimed at how to present information, not how to listen to it. As a result, teachers are often talking in the classroom when they should be listening.

Becky tries to remember that she must be silent in order to create opportunities for children to converse. If she responds to everything that is said, children tend to talk through her rather than with one another. If children don't have time to talk with one another, they will not know how to listen to and learn from their peers. Having a teacher who always directs the conversations does not empower students. Over time, they learn to be more passive, to wait until they are told what to do and what to think.

Even short silences make a difference. Becky doesn't always wait long enough after she asks a question, even though she knows that a longer *wait time* (the pause after a question) increases the number and the quality of responses (Rowe 1986). Waiting just three to five seconds results in significantly improved discussions. Becky also tries to wait for several responses to a question, because this lets children know there is more than one possible response and encourages them to keep thinking. It breaks down the alternating speaking pattern of teacher, student, teacher, student, teacher, student.

Listening is more than just being silent and making meaning out of the words one hears, however. Becky also tries to notice tone of voice, speed of articulation, facial expressions, and body language. Changes in any of these characteristics are often cues about what's happening to a child emotionally. Sometimes listening means noticing that a child looks down when he isn't sure of his answer. Sometimes it means noticing that a child talks very quickly when she has just made a new discovery. Information like this helps Becky respond better to her students' needs.

As an active listener Becky encourages her students to speak by showing she is interested in what they are saying. She nods her head and leans forward, makes supportive comments (*Yes, Oh, I see*), and probes deeper by asking children to elaborate. Interest like this demonstrates that she cares about her students and is curious about their thinking. It is also important for Becky to let children know that she understands what is said. She often restates what she hears as a way to check for meaning and builds on a child's comments by referring to them in her own statements.

For many teachers, the most difficult listening skill is giving their undivided attention. It is often a challenge to concentrate exclusively on one child within a busy classroom. With practice, however, it does get easier. We all need to remember that no one likes to talk to someone whose eyes are darting all over the place and whose attention is clearly wandering.

Becky also lets her students know that she wants to remember what they say. She keeps a clipboard handy for jotting down notes during the day. Initially many children respond warily. They want to know what she is writing. As they get more familiar with the practice, they react with pride; their words are being recorded. Before long they announce, *Get your clipboard. I'm going to say something important!*

As part of her professional development, Becky has gathered data directly from her classroom. She has tape-recorded a discussion in order to find out how often she speaks, how long her wait time is, and how she communicates to students that she values their comments. She has taken notes during a whole-class or small-group discussion about who talks, how often they talk, what their gender is, and where they are sitting. She has invited a colleague to observe math talk in her classroom and give her feedback. She has had her classroom videotaped so that she can see her nonverbal behavior. Examining things like these isn't always easy, but it does provide her with important insights into her ability to encourage and support discourse.

Students as Listeners

Students need to be active listeners as well. Teachers need to encourage listening skills early on so that they become a habit, an expectation of the classroom. The most important things we can do to improve our students' listening skills are to:

- Model good listening skills ourselves.
- Provide students with appropriate opportunities to practice their ability to listen.
- Let children know that we expect them to practice good listening habits and help them understand what it means to do so.
- Communicate effectively so that listening is rewarded.

It is difficult for young children to sit still for very long and to function well in large groups. Over time, however, children in kindergarten can learn to be attentive. For example, one day in late January, Becky's class is learning about the traditions and customs associated with Chinese New Year. Ana's mom has come to class to share family stories about the holiday. The children are also fascinated by the dragon dance they see on a video. They are impressed by the large mask and giggle because they can only see people's legs and feet. The children are naturally curious about the number of legs they can see, and lots of them are counting to themselves. Becky decides to take advantage of their interest.

BECKY: LET'S PRETEND THAT WE ARE ALL PART OF THE DANCE. LET'S SIT IN A CIRCLE AND STRETCH OUR LEGS INTO THE MIDDLE. HOW MANY LEGS DOES OUR DRAGON HAVE?

LISA: Twenty-three.

RORY: I agree.

ALLISON: That can't be right. There are twenty-three people. No, twenty-four, with Miss Eston, and twenty-five, with Ana's mom. There has to be more, because everyone has two legs. [*The children seem puzzled. Many were satisfied when twenty-three was offered as a solution, but Allison's additional reasoning has posed a problem. Becky waits, but no one offers another prediction.*]

BECKY: [*Asking a question to keep the children focused on the task*] HOW COULD WE SOLVE THIS PROBLEM?

HALEY: We could count.

CHARLIE: Yeah, let's count. [*Many children start counting simultaneously. There is lots of commotion and confusion.*]

TREVOR: This doesn't work. Can we do it one at a time?

BECKY: WHAT DO OTHERS THINK ABOUT TREVOR'S SUGGESTION?

KAITLIN: I think it's a good idea.

BECKY: HOW SHOULD WE START?

NICOLE: I'll start. One. [*There is a long pause. Nicole looks at Allison, who is sitting next to her. Allison looks right back at Nicole.*]

ALLISON: You have to say two.

NICOLE: No, I said one. You are two.

ALLISON: No, you have to say one and two. We are counting our legs. See [*she touches each of her legs*], one, two.

NICOLE: [*Touching each of her legs*] One, two.

ALLISON:	Three, four.
JAMAL:	Five, six,
TREVOR:	Seven, eight.
SAMMY:	Nine, ten.
LISA:	Eleven, twelve.
TANYA:	Thirteen, fourteen. [*The counting continues as expected until it is Charlie's turn.*]
CHARLIE:	Twenty-nine, twenty-ten. [*Ben, whose turn is next, does not continue counting. After a moment, Charlie giggles and buries his face in his hands.*] I mean thirty.
BEN:	Thirty-one, thirty-two. [*The counting continues.*]

While they are counting, the children listen carefully to each other. Their eyes move attentively from one speaker to the next. The way children react to the errors of other children is particularly noteworthy. Allison challenges the predictions of Lisa and Rory and objects to Nicole's counting. Ben remains silent after Charlie's "twenty-ten," which gives Charlie time to correct himself. In no case is it necessary for Becky to intervene; the children handle it themselves. No one speaks out of turn.

When the children finish, there are lots of smiles. They seem proud of their collaborative work and aware that they have completed a complex task. Alone, most of them would not have been able to answer this question correctly. Together, they have been successful.

Children do not always listen so well: *They never listen to directions* and *They never pay attention* are common teacher laments, the underlying message being that there is something wrong with the children. While many factors in today's society have lessened children's ability to listen effectively, as teachers we need to examine our own behavior as well.

Becky uses classroom routines to increase the likelihood that children will listen. Following a noisy workshop or a physical activity, she often leads the students in singing a song as a way to help them refocus. She gives clear directions and uses simple visual aids that help the children remember each step in a procedure. She encourages children to rephrase her directions, asking *Who can tell me what to do first?* She avoids repeating directions several times and unintentionally giving children the message that they don't need to listen the first time.

Becky also wants to help children understand what it means to be a good listener. She talks with them about what a good listener does so that they can begin to associate this skill with concrete behavior. She records their ideas about listening on chart paper (see Figure 5.1) and adds to this list during several similar conversations over the course of the year so that the children can refine their understanding.

Finally, Becky provides opportunities for children to practice their ability to listen:

- She has children close their eyes and visualize a short story as she tells it.
- During discussions she asks students to restate the comments of other students, refers student questions to other students, and asks students whether they agree or disagree with comments they hear.
- She plays the game Telephone with the children.

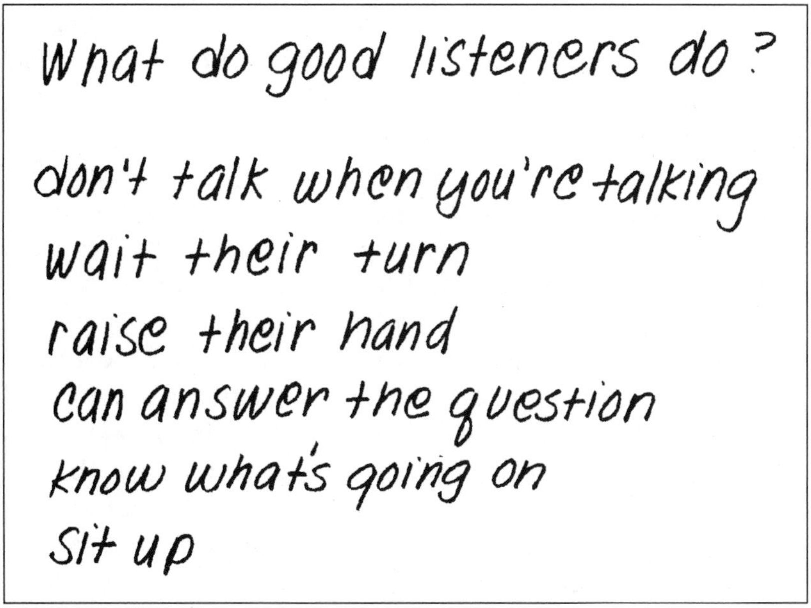

What do good listeners do?

don't talk when you're talking
wait their turn
raise their hand
can answer the question
know what's going on
sit up

FIGURE 5.1 Becky's class chart listing the behavior of good listeners

- She plays a game in which she asks children to follow two or three simple directions—*touch your nose, clap your hands,* and *stamp your feet,* for example. All of the directions are given at once, before the activities are performed, in order to encourage auditory memory. (Sometimes Becky asks a child to give the initial directions, because she wants to make sure the children have as many opportunities to listen to one another as to her.)
- She reads aloud to her students every day.

Reflective Conversations

As children become better listeners, they are more able to participate in group conversations about their learning. Some educators believe that such participation is beyond the reach of children in kindergarten. Becky disagrees. Reflection is an essential part of learning at all levels, and kindergarten children should be encouraged and guided to undertake it. It can be invaluable to the intellectual growth of both students and teachers.

When students reflect about what they have learned, they think back on their experiences. Probing questions are often required to stimulate this kind of thinking. Asking *Why did you do that?* or *How is this like what you did yesterday?* helps students review what they have done. When Becky asks *How did you build this?* or *What did you do first?* she encourages students to step back and look at things again, to consider other perspectives. Even if children respond *I don't know,* they have stopped to think for a moment and understand that she views such analysis as part of the learning process. In time, the I-don't-know responses are interspersed with descriptions of their actions, predictions of outcomes, and explanations of what they found.

Reflective thinking is also encouraged through debriefing sessions. Few kindergarten teachers hold sessions like this with the whole class. Becky first became interested in large-group debriefing sessions after observing writing workshop in her colleague Marie Crispen's first-grade classroom. She saw children sitting in a circle, sharing their writing one at a time. As each child spoke, the other children listened and then responded to what they heard. Becky's reaction? "Kindergarten children can do this, too!"

She began by following a similar procedure. For example, when her students drew pictures of things that come in twos, she had them bring their pictures to a class meeting and share them one by one. Later, she explored other debriefing formats. When children explored problems with multiple answers (*There are six shapes on the table. Some shapes are squares and some shapes are triangles. How many of each shape are on the table?*), she had them discuss their answers. When a solution was given Becky asked, "Does anyone else have that answer, too?" This type of sharing is more natural then going around the circle one by one. It offers the children a chance to make connections and better holds their attention.

Becky also has children talk as a whole group about their strategies. In one activity that Becky uses, children count varying quantities of keys in different bags and then decide whether there are more than, less than, or exactly five keys. Then the children gather in a circle.

BECKY:	WHO CAN TELL ME WHAT WE JUST DID?
KIMI:	We counted keys.
JOSÉ:	We matched to five.
NICOLE:	Sometimes I got more than five.
MARIO:	Sometimes less.
KAITLIN:	I got five once.
BECKY:	HOW DID YOU COUNT THE KEYS IN YOUR BAG?
MEI:	I went, one, two, three . . .
BECKY:	COULD YOU SHOW US WHAT YOU DID?
MEI:	Can I get a bag of keys?
BECKY:	YES.
MEI:	[*Quickly getting a bag, dumping the keys on the rug in front of her, and touching them one by one as she counts*] One, two, three, four, five, six. Six is more than five.
JAMAL:	Mei touched the keys to count. I do that, too.
BECKY:	HOW MANY OF YOU TOUCH THE KEYS AS YOU SAY THE NUMBERS? [*Most hands go up.*] WOULD ANYONE ELSE LIKE TO SHOW US HOW YOU COUNTED? [*Several hands go up.*] BEN?
BEN:	[*Suiting his actions to his words*] I take one out and count it. Then I take another one out and count it. Then I count them altogether at the end. I got five.

RORY: Ben counts twice.

LISA: I do that sometimes.

BEN: It helps me be sure.

MEGAN: Can I show you my way now? [*Becky nods. Megan takes the bag and two of the keys from Ben.*] I have two. That's less than five.

BECKY: HOW DID YOU KNOW THERE WERE TWO?

MEGAN: When there's that many, I just see it.

Through this conversation, the children learn about one another's strategies. They are exposed to new ways of thinking. They learn that some of their classmates do things the same way that they do. Their math talk involves gesturing, touching objects, and dramatizing ideas. These motions help children remember what they did and communicate the process to others.

Becky works hard not to underestimate her young students' abilities to participate in reflective conversations. She has this advice for teachers who want to encourage similar conversations:

- Begin with small-group reflections. Children will have greater opportunities to participate and will learn skills they can use later in larger groups.
- Keep conversations short in the beginning. Children will be able to engage in longer conversations as they practice their abilities to talk and listen.
- Involve all the children at once, but give them individual materials to interact with as they converse. Having children dramatize the counting process in pairs doesn't allow children to view more than one other person's strategies, but it does help them stay involved and remain focused.
- Don't respond to every comment. Encourage the children to talk to one another directly.
- Ask questions that allow for several responses. Once several replies are made, ask a question that encourages children to think about the answers given (*How did you get these answers? How are your answers alike? different?*).

Monitoring group conversations is complex. Becky needs to decide when to intervene, which ideas to pursue, when to encourage participation, and when to provide additional information or guidance. Most important, she must find an appropriate balance between meeting each child's needs and meeting the needs of the group as a whole.

Sometimes a child tells a rather long and detailed story, and the other children begin to fidget. Then Becky intervenes in order to keep the group on task. A comment like *Your story is so exciting. Would you save the rest of it for snack time?* allows her to intercede without making the child feel unappreciated. When a child habitually talks too long, Becky speaks to him or her privately. She explains that other children sometimes find it hard to listen to one person for a long time, even when that person is saying something interesting. She then asks *Do you think you took turns talking today?* to help the child learn to judge his or her own behavior.

Conversely, Becky also worries about the children who are too shy to speak comfortably in front of a group or whose language or speech development makes it difficult for them to do so. Inviting such children ahead of time to share their ideas in the upcoming meeting can be very helpful. Giving them an opportunity to rehearse is beneficial as well. The examples below are comments Becky uses to support children who are less comfortable talking in a group:

- You have been working hard on your pattern. I like the way you check to make sure that the square-triangle-circle pattern is repeated. Would you be willing to show your pattern during meeting time and talk about how you made it?
- Tomorrow it is your turn to be the daily helper. Would you like to practice the morning routines today?
- You just explained what you did very well. Would you be willing to tell Orin and Lisa what you just told me?

In each case, Becky phrases her suggestion so that the child has the right to decline. Her job is to encourage and provide support for participation, not to demand it.

Placing this kind of emphasis on language is also a concern for teachers with students who are emergent English speakers. When the sole focus of the mathematics curriculum is computation, that curriculum is basically free of cultural bias. But computation skills are only one aspect of mathematics. What happens in an idea-based curriculum that requires children to speak, listen, read, and write about mathematical ideas? According to Leslie Garrison,

> Although the [NCTM] standards' emphasis on language may appear to put the learning of emergent English speakers at risk, these standards are actually in alignment with current teaching strategies in bilingual education. Sound bilingual instructional practices encourage students to work in groups, promote a curriculum relevant to students' experiences, and stress thinking skills. (1997, p.132)

Becky tries to remember that mathematics vocabulary can present particular challenges. There are a variety of terms for the same concept (*add, sum, combine, plus,* and *join,* for example). Also, some words, like *table,* have a mathematical and a nonmathematical meaning. Though these variations can be problematic for all students, they may be especially so for those who are not yet proficient English speakers (Olivares 1996). For example, in Spanish a mathematical table is a *tabla,* and a different word is used to name a piece of furniture. Because English instruction does not usually include mathematical vocabulary, a picture dictionary can be helpful. Thinking carefully about the specialized vocabulary of particular math tasks helps Becky identify terms to explore with emergent English speakers in advance. (Chapter 6 discusses mathematical terms in more detail.)

Problem contexts can also present cultural barriers. Connecting tasks to classroom events and thematic units helps ensure that children understand problem settings. Becky also makes a point to celebrate various cultures within her classroom, and she encourages students who are learning English to count and name shapes in their first language and to teach their classmates to do so, too.

Pictorial representations give children less proficient in English an opportunity to explain their thinking. Often other children are the best helpers. When children with the same first language work together, they can discuss their mathematical ideas in that language. Sometimes, a student proficient in

English will become a personal translator. A pair may form that works together for several weeks. Becky is grateful for such teams.

Many standard procedures in the kindergarten classroom are helpful to non–English speakers. Manipulatives, pictures, diagrams, and body language are used frequently to communicate ideas. Concepts are explored before they are linked to symbolic representations. Dramatizations and concrete materials help all students understand concepts and identify word meanings. The whole class is introduced to new ideas at the same time.

The Mystery Box

In many kindergarten classrooms, Show and Tell has traditionally been used to promote language development, since it lets children practice the art of discourse. Each child is encouraged to bring a familiar item to school, and time is set aside for the children to show and tell about these favorite things. Over the years, however, Becky has found that Show and Tell poses problems. Sometimes the children are competitive about what they have to share. Some children are distracted throughout the day by what they have brought to present. Becky feels these negative byproducts outweigh other positive contributions. Also, Show and Tell is very time-consuming. Therefore, when a friend's five-year-old told Becky about a special box he was using in his classroom, a new and very purposeful activity was born.

Beginning in mid-October, Becky adds the Mystery Box to the routines of the morning meeting. Each day the daily helper is given a shoe box to take home. With the help of his or her parents or guardian, the child chooses an item to put into the box, something she or he wants to share with the class: a special toy, an artifact from nature, a souvenir, a book, a postcard, a photograph. Then the child and his or her family write out three clues about what the item is and tape them to the top of the box. The next day the child shares the clues with the class and calls on classmates to make guesses. This process provides opportunities for children to get to know one another better, to celebrate what is important to one member of the community, and to do some deductive reasoning. It also gives two children the opportunity to lead class activities each day.

When it is Trevor's turn, on a day in early January, he holds the Mystery Box tightly closed and announces his first clue.

TREVOR: It is white and fuzzy. [*Many hands go up. Trevor begins to call on individual classmates.*] Mei?

MEI: A Beanie Baby bunny?

TREVOR: No. Jamal?

JAMAL: A Beanie Baby sheep?

TREVOR: No. Kimi?

KIMI: A lamb?

JAMAL: A lamb is a sheep.

TREVOR: It's not a lamb. Charlie?

CHARLIE: A Beanie Baby polar bear?

TREVOR: No. Haley?

HALEY: Is it an animal?[2]

TREVOR: Yes. Sammy?

SAMMY: A seal?

TREVOR: No. Rosita?

ROSITA: [*Sensing that it's time for more information*] What's the next clue?

TREVOR: People are scared of this. [*More hands shoot up.*] Mario?

MARIO: A monster?

SAMMY: Monsters aren't white and fluffy.

HALEY: The abominable snowman is.

KIMI: That can't fit in the box.

TANYA: A toy one can.

TREVOR: No, it's not the abominable snowman. Ezra?

EZRA: A ghost?

---

[2]Children often begin to ask questions, rather than just make another guess, as a way to narrow the field of choices. It is also natural for them to interject comments without being called on as a way of talking through the process. The discussion becomes more of a conversation than a call-and-response session. The children are usually able to monitor this process on their own and return to raising their hands when they have new guesses to contribute.

MEGAN:	It can't be a ghost. They aren't fluffy.
TREVOR:	No, it's not a ghost. [*He looks around. No hands are raised. After looking at Becky for a moment, he reads the third clue.*]
TREVOR:	It has a long tail.
ANA:	A fox?
SAMMY:	People aren't scared of foxes.
ALLISON:	They might be. But a fox isn't white.
TREVOR:	It's not a fox. Kaitlin?
KAITLIN:	A white squirrel?
TREVOR:	No. Squirrels aren't white.
KAITLIN:	They might be.
TREVOR:	Rory?
RORY:	A rat.
TREVOR:	No, but that's close. [*Many more hands go up.*]
HALEY:	A mouse?
MANY VOICES:	That's what I was going to say.
TREVOR:	Yup. It's a mouse. [*He opens the Mystery Box and shows everyone his toy mouse.*]

This discussion is fairly typical for midyear. The children are easily engaged with the task of figuring out the clues and listen attentively to one another. They can have a Mystery Box discussion on their own without an adult's acting as a catalyst for each step of the conversation. It is important for children to learn that they can monitor their own discussions. It is one more way to demystify the role of teacher.

In this case, the children do not always combine the clues; their deductive reasoning falls in and out of play, which is typical. For example, when the second clue is given the children concentrate solely on the attribute of scariness and forget that the mystery object is an animal. Nevertheless, talking about the Mystery Box each day gives the children opportunities to develop their language abilities and to focus on the exchange of ideas. They also begin to develop deductive reasoning and other higher-level thinking skills, which are powerful tools in mathematical thinking.

Developing conversation skills with a group of young children can be difficult. So often the dialogue seesaws back and forth between one child, the teacher, and then another child. The teacher often becomes the interpreter. For Becky, activities like the Mystery Box promote natural dialogues among children and lay the foundation for other types of discussions. Children begin to feel comfortable with the exchange process and to recognize the need to listen to one another. They also learn to challenge one another's ideas. It is not unusual for them to correct one another during the exchange if a guess does not meet the current clue or when a guess is repeated. Over time, the children apply these talking and listening habits to their mathematical conversations as well.

6

Weaving Mathematics
and Literature

Of all the connections between language and mathematics, teachers are probably most familiar with using children's literature to teach mathematical ideas. More than a decade ago, Becky began exploring ways literature can promote mathematical thinking.

There are a variety of reasons to use children's literature to teach mathematics. For one thing, the characters and settings in a story provide a context in which mathematical thinking feels authentic. Then too, literature captures students' interest and imagination, and this enthusiam can be highly motivational. Also important, interdisciplinary teaching allows a more holistic approach to learning. Finally, reading good books with children is enjoyable.

Becky often uses the chapter "A Lost Button," in *Frog and Toad Are Friends* (Lobel 1970), or *The Button Box* (Reid 1990) to introduce a sorting unit. Sometimes she reads a story at the end of an investigation, to give closure. For example, after a counting activity she may read *The Midnight Farm* (Lindbergh 1987). In the story, a mother and child take a tour of a farm at midnight. They count groups of animals, from one to ten, as they walk around the farm. The rich language and muted illustrations present a safe and harmonious world and project a quiet peace.

Becky also uses literature to provide a context for mathematical explorations and to expose children to the language and pictures of mathematics. Good literature often becomes the basis for one- or two-week thematic adventures. What's most important is that the literature launch or solidify, not replace, the mathematical activity.

Counting Books

There are usually a variety of counting books in kindergarten classrooms. While we all have our favorites, it is important to understand the mathematical differences among them and how they can best be used. Counting books like *Counting Wildflowers* (McMillan 1986) are picture books with few, if any, words. Books like *The Very Hungry Caterpillar* (Carle 1989) have a simple story line and are often repetitive and predictable. Predictable story lines allow children to participate quickly in telling and retelling the story.

Ten, Nine, Eight (Bang 1983) begins at ten and counts backward. *Seven Eggs* (Hopper 1985) doesn't start or end with ten. *How Many Feet in the Bed?* (Hamm 1991) and *What Comes in 2's, 3's, & 4's?* (Aker 1990) focus on one-to-many correspondence. *One Watermelon Seed* (Barker 1985) counts to ten by ones and then counts by tens. *Frog Counts to Ten* (Liebler 1994) is a story as well as a counting book. Reading or being read these books, children practice counting forward and backward, predict the number that comes next without saying the whole counting sequence, associate groups of things with their corresponding numerals, and see examples of numbers in the real world.

One Gorilla

When reading counting books to children, we have the opportunity to make the counting process explicit and teach important skills. Consider *One Gorilla* (Morozumi 1990), which lists the animals the author of the book loves. The number of each animal on the list increases by one. The animals, shown on beautiful two-page illustrations, are scattered about, so keeping track of which ones have been counted is a challenge. (The single gorilla is part of each grouping.) Becky has previously read the book with the whole class, and it has been available for children to explore on their own. Today she is rereading the book with a group of six children to help them focus on their counting skills.

BECKY: "EIGHT FISH IN THE SEA AND ONE GORILLA." WHO CAN FIND THE GORILLA?

LISA: Me. It's on the rock.

BECKY: LET'S COUNT THE FISH.

EVERYONE: One, two, three, four—

BECKY: WAIT A MINUTE. DID WE COUNT THIS ONE BEFORE? I CAN'T REMEMBER.

BEN: I think we did.

RORY: I'm not sure.

BECKY: IS IT IMPORTANT TO KNOW WHICH FISH WE'VE COUNTED?

HALEY: Yes.

BECKY: WHY?

LISA: So we don't count them more than once.

BEN: So we get them all.

BECKY: HOW COULD WE BE SURE TO COUNT EACH ONE EXACTLY ONCE?

KAITLIN: We could cover them up after.

LISA: We could go in order.

CHARLIE: [*Pointing to the top of the left page and moving his hand to the bottom of the right page*] Like start here and count to here.

Used in this way, counting books do more than expose children to numbers in the real world and encourage them to practice the counting sequence. They allow them to develop ideas and skills related to one-to-one correspondence and keeping track of what is counted. When children interact with a story as it is reread, they are able to see strategies in action and try them out personally.

Learning the necessity of keeping track of what has been counted is an important concept in kindergarten. Once children understand the importance of keeping track, they need to develop techniques for doing so. It's easier for young children to keep track of concrete objects. They can pick the objects up or move them to show that they have been counted. Pictures of objects are static and thus more problematic. Counting books provide opportunities for a teacher to focus on this important skill. Too often, the teacher merely counts correctly. However, Becky chooses to accentuate the point of keeping track by asking, "Did we count this one before?"

Ten Black Dots

While all counting books expose children to words, symbols, or pictures related to number, particular children and teachers gravitate toward particular books and illustrations. Becky's favorite illustration is in the book *Ten Black Dots* (Crews 1986). The book begins with the question "What can you do with ten black dots?" Colorful illustrations, one for each of the numbers one through ten, portray that number of "dots" in an everyday setting. The two-page illustration for the number six shows a left hand and a right hand, each a different color and each holding three "marbles." Every time Becky reads the story to a class, some child almost always says, "Three plus three makes six," when Becky holds up this picture. It's a great lead-in to, "What else makes six?" and often prompts this investigation.

In first or second grade this book can be the basis of the question *How many black dots are there in all?* In kindergarten, however, it is more appropriate to focus on the counting sequence and the circular shapes of everyday objects. Becky used to ask the children to make their own pictures for the story. Unfortunately, students too often deferred to the illustrations in the book rather than creating new ideas. In order to tap her students' imagination, she now asks them to make illustrations for a new story, "Ten Black Squares." They may use examples from the story to stimulate their thinking, but they are no longer able to replicate the work exactly.

Each child makes an illustration for one of the numbers from one through ten. Becky does not assign the children numbers, and she makes more than enough one-and-a-half-inch black squares available. Some children start with a drawing (often of a house or building), then add the squares later (as doors and windows, for example). Others take one or two squares, glue them on their paper, and create a picture around them. Allison starts with a single square and creates a jack-in-the-box (see Figure 6.1). Kaitlin begins with two squares and uses them for the eyes of a dog (see Figure 6.2). Ben makes a bus with the squares as wheels (see Figure 6.3). Sammy sees the bus and exclaims, "Your bus has flat tires!" Ben laughs. "I guess I was thinking about dots."

Other children manipulate the squares on their white paper to see what they can construct without adding details with crayons. Their illustrations often turn out to be towers or stairs. Lisa declares, "Ten squares make a staircase. See four, three, two, one." As she speaks she moves her finger across each row of her staircase, starting at the bottom row. She then records the number

FIGURE 6.1 Allison's jack-in-the-box

FIGURE 6.2 Kaitlin's dog

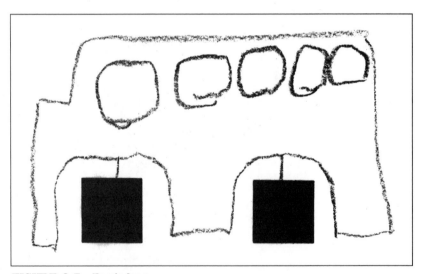

FIGURE 6.3 Ben's bus

of squares at the end of the rows. Recounting her squares, she writes *10* at the top of the staircase. (See Figure 6.4.) Rory makes a tower (see Figure 6.5). He counts the squares several times but does not record any numbers.

Becky is amazed at the variety of ways in which children approach open-ended tasks like this one. Something always happens that she would not have predicted. For example, today Tanya has made a house and is about to use her squares for windows, but she hesitates. Then she takes a pair of scissors from the work can she is using, cuts a square in half, and positions her windows (see Figure 6.6). To some teachers, this would be a problem. After all, the lesson's focus is on squares. But Becky finds Tanya's adaptation intriguing. She doesn't say anything to Tanya right away, however, because she doesn't want her to feel self-conscious or to suggest to the other children that they should change the way they are working.

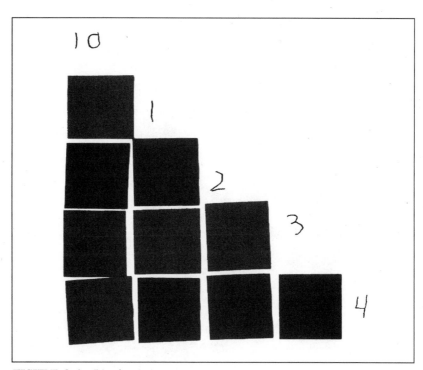

FIGURE 6.4 Lisa's staircase

FIGURE 6.5   Rory's tower

FIGURE 6.6   Tanya's house

Later, Becky asks Tanya about her work. Tanya responds, "I wanted my windows to be smaller. See, if you cut a square here you get two rectangles." Tanya has certainly learned something about squares, and Becky feels the rationale behind her decision to make materials in the work cans available to students at all times has been reinforced.

What Comes in 2's, 3's & 4's?

A particular book can become the basis for a weeklong exploration, as *What Comes in 2's, 3's & 4's?* (Aker 1990) does when Becky introduces it one morning. The book focuses on things that come in groups. It begins with the number two and points out a number of things (eyes, ears, arms, hands, legs, etc.) that come in groups of two. Then it does the same for the numbers three and four. The children are excited when Becky brings the book to the meeting area.

BECKY: I HAVE A NEW BOOK TO SHARE TO START MATH WORKSHOP TODAY. WHAT DO YOU NOTICE ABOUT THE COVER?

TANYA: I see numbers . . . two, three, and four.

ALLISON: I see shapes.

JAMAL: I see an eight.

BECKY: CAN YOU TELL US MORE?

JAMAL: Right there with the two, three, and four.

TREVOR: It's an and.

BECKY: YES, I SEE THAT NOW. ACTUALLY, THAT IS A SYMBOL THAT MEANS *AND*. SOMETIMES AUTHORS USE THIS SYMBOL INSTEAD OF SPELLING OUT A-N-D. IT DOES LOOK LIKE AN EIGHT. BUT WHEN WE READ THIS IT SAYS TWOS, THREES, AND FOURS.

BEN: I see a traffic light.

MEGAN: And a cat and a dog.

EZRA: There's an airplane.

TREVOR: A bird.

SAMMY: I see an ice cream cone—I mean a piece of pizza.

ALLISON: There are Ss.

NICOLE: A question mark is at the end.

BECKY: YES, THERE IS A QUESTION MARK. IT GOES WITH THE TITLE OF THE BOOK. THIS SAYS [*pointing to the words*], "WHAT COMES IN TWOS, THREES, AND FOURS?" [*There is a bit of a silence.*] WHAT

DOES IT MEAN, "WHAT COMES IN TWOS, THREES, AND FOURS?" [*The children continue to respond with things they notice about the cover. No one seems willing or able to answer the question.*] SO WHAT DO YOU THINK THIS BOOK IS ABOUT? WHAT IS THE AUTHOR ASKING US?

NICOLE: I think numbers.

TALI: I think it's an I Spy game.

EZRA: Altogether it [2 + 3 + 4] makes nine.

BECKY: TALI HAS SUGGESTED THAT THIS IS LIKE AN I SPY GAME. LET'S SEE IF WE CAN SPY SOMETHING THAT COMES IN TWOS.

MEGAN: Birds.

BECKY: CAN YOU SAY MORE?

MEGAN: A mom and a dad bird.

TREVOR: A sister and a brother bird.

BECKY: WHAT ELSE COMES IN TWOS?

ALLISON: Twins.

BEN: Owls . . . one is a daddy owl and one is a mommy owl.

HALEY: Two wings on a bird.

EZRA: But there are lots of feathers.

ANA: Two hands and two feet.

EZRA: Ten fingers.

TANYA: Two ears and two eyes.

JAMAL: Two legs.

MEGAN: A pair of shoes is two shoes.

SAMMY: Two arms.

BEN: Two nose holes.

TREVOR: A cat and a dog.

ALLISON: Can we start on with the book?

It is important to expose children to the idea that some items come in sets or groups. Focusing on common pairs is the initial step. Becky asks the children to spy something that comes in twos to build on Tali's comment and to let children begin by making observations. At first it is difficult for Becky to focus the children's attention on the mathematics of what comes in groups of two. The pivotal point is Haley's suggestion that a bird has two wings. Other responses follow quickly. Allison's closing comment simply reminds Becky that conversations should not take up too much time. Often it is hard to create just the right balance.

Next the class reads the book in its entirety. The children are delighted when they notice that the author has included some of the same responses they have given. Afterward, Becky gives the children paper so that they can answer the question *What comes in 2's?* in their own way. At first many children struggle with what it means to be a group or set. They are quick to generate answers like two jelly beans or two bunnies. Becky encourages them to think of things that almost always come in pairs. This can be a big leap for many children. It is always a challenge for Becky to know just how much she can expect. Figure 6.7 is Ben's drawing of things that come in twos.

Becky had thought the mathematical concepts in this book would be explored for just a day or two. The children, however, have other ideas. As the days go by, many of them return to the

FIGURE 6.7   Ben's drawing of things that come in twos

FIGURE 6.8   Things that come in groups

idea of what comes in groups. Working individually and in small groups, they generate more ideas. Responses become as unique and sophisticated as "Two shapes in a pattern" and "Two halves to a moon." Some children explore additional numbers. Finally, at the end of the week, they display posters of their work (see Figure 6.8 for a sample.)

Developing Vocabulary

Children's literature is an ideal vehicle for exposing children to the vocabulary of mathematics. The mathematics curriculum includes many specific terms used to designate properties, label objects, describe relationships, name motions, and delineate transformations. Consider the following examples of terms used in kindergarten classrooms:

Position: *over, under, down, around, up, next to, between, top, bottom, in, on, right, left, before, after, first, second, third, last*

Comparison: *longer, shorter, heavier, lighter, bigger, smaller, greater than, less than, more, fewer, the same as, equal to, different from*

Quantity: *lots, many, few, most, one, two, three*

Duration: *second, minute, hour, day, week, month, year*

Combination: *put together, in all, altogether, add, collect, put in*

Separation: *cut, break, take away, pull out, divide*

Geometry: *round, straight, line, curve, triangle, square, circle, cube, cone*

Kindergartners should not be expected to learn formal definitions of these terms, but they need to become familiar with them and with the concepts they represent. It is difficult to learn vocabulary that is rarely used or that is unconnected to some other form of understanding. It is much easier if the terms are encountered within a natural, meaningful context like a story.

Tana Hoban has published several "photo essays" that promote discussions involving mathematical terms. *All About Where* (1991) uses positional language in the picture descriptions. *Push–Pull, Empty–Full* (1972) focuses on opposites. Many of the pairs of words in the latter book have mathematical significance (*light, heavy* and *many, few,* for example).

Billy's Button, by William Accorsi (1992), also fosters positional language. Billy's button is talked about and shown in a variety of settings. The repeated question "Where is Billy's button?" encourages children to describe where the button is in the illustrations. Most children just want to point to the pictures, but Becky encourages them to use words as well.

Often when Becky reads books like this to her students, she follows up with activities designed to encourage them to recognize and use specific terms. Here are some examples:

- Playing a game of Simon Says that incorporates specific positional language: "Put your hand on top of your head."

- Playing a game of I Spy in which children must give positional clues: "It's behind you."
- Singing "Hokey Pokey" and encouraging the children to dramatize the meaning of *in, out, around, right,* and *left.*
- Using ordinal numbers and terms like *last, first, behind, in front of,* and *between* when the children are lining up to go somewhere.
- Dramatizing songs and chants that incorporate ordinal numbers.

Activities like this are easily incorporated into the classroom routine, often as transitions between longer activities.

Becky also has children work in pairs with a barrier between them so they can't see each other. They take turns giving directions for building a four-color Unifix cube tower, for example, or a figure on the geoboard, or a design made with five pattern blocks. Children enjoy these copycat activities, and the activities prompt further discussion.

For example, Tali builds a cube tower and gives directions to Megan so that she can build an identical one. After Tali finishes her directions, the girls remove the barrier between them and compare their structures:

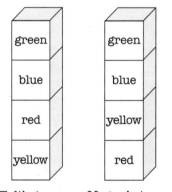

Tali's tower   Megan's tower

Then they negotiate the meaning of the term *under.*

MEGAN:	How come they're not the same? You told me to put the yellow one under the blue one.
TALI:	It is.
MEGAN:	No, the red one is.
TALI:	The yellow one is too.
MEGAN:	The yellow one is under the red one.
TALI:	It's under the red and blue and green.
MEGAN:	That's not fair.

The Bus Stop

Many children's stories beg to be read over and over. Often this rereading encourages children to dramatize the story. In *The Bus Stop* (Hellen 1988), first one person comes to wait for the bus, then another and another, until seven people are in line. After each person's position in line is identified, there is the repeated question, "But can you see the bus yet?" An ingenious illustration brings the story to a delightful and surprising conclusion: the last page depicts a bus with cutout windows; when this page is superimposed on the previous page, the seven people's faces are seen through the windows as if they have boarded the bus.

Becky first reads this story early in the year, and the children are captivated by the simple plot and the vivid illustrations. They ask to hear the story over and over. Becky decides to have the children dramatize the story, because it will give them more experience with ordinal numbers. She makes a bus-stop sign and posts it in the meeting area. Next she cuts out seven drawings of buses and tapes each one to the end of a tongue depressor so that the children can hold them up easily. On both sides of each bus she writes one of the numerals one through seven.

Before she reads *The Bus Stop* the next morning, she distributes the seven buses to seven children. Then she says, "I need you to listen carefully to the story again today. When you think the number on your bus matches the order in which the person I am reading about arrives at the bus stop, I want you to come and stand by the bus-stop sign."

Once she is sure these directions are understood, Becky begins to read. Since the children have already heard the story a few times, they chime in with "But can you see the bus yet?" when the first person arrives at the bus stop. At the same time, Trevor (who is holding bus 1) gets up, walks over to the sign on the wall, and stands there. The story continues, and the children with bus 2 and bus 3 stand and join the line in the appropriate order. Then Becky reads the part where the fourth and fifth persons, a parent and child, join the bus line simultaneously. This time no one moves.

SAMMY: Who is next?

JAMAL: We need the fourth and fifth person.

ALLISON: Who has number four?

HALEY: Yeah, and number five.

Everyone looks at the remaining buses. Finally Ana and Mario stand up. Ana's sign has a four on it, Mario's, a five. Both children move to get in line. Mario stands next to Mei, who has the sign with the number three. Ana stands on the other side of Mario. Becky hesitates. She is tempted to interrupt and correct the situation but decides to finish the story. "Sixth . . . ," reads Becky, and Tanya stands up. When Becky reads, "Seventh . . . ," Rory joins the line, standing before Trevor, who is first. Seven children are now facing the class. The order on the busses they hold reads: 7, 1, 2, 3, 5, 4, 6.

BECKY: LET'S LOOK AT THE PEOPLE FROM OUR CLASS WHO ARE WAITING FOR THE BUS.

ALLISON: That's not right.

KAITLIN: They're out of order.

BECKY: WHAT DO YOU MEAN, THEY ARE OUT OF ORDER?

JAMAL: The numbers aren't right.

NICOLE: I think Mario and Ana need to switch.

JAMAL: And number seven has to be after number six.

BECKY: LET'S SEE WHAT HAPPENS WHEN THESE SUGGESTIONS ARE FOLLOWED. NICOLE SAID THAT MARIO AND ANA NEED TO SWITCH PLACES, AND JAMAL SAID THAT SEVEN COMES AFTER SIX. [*Mario and Ana switch places, and Rory moves to the end of the line.*]

ALLISON: Now that's better.

This simple dramatization allows the children to talk about number order and to solve a problem within a context. However, now all the other children want their turn to "be in the play." Becky agrees they can dramatize the story again just before going home, so that seven more children can take part. She adds, "I'll leave the book and all the bus signs here in the meeting area. You can give it a try on your own as well, during exploration."

Some children act out the story on their own, retelling it as best they can. Others get a turn at the end of the day. There is only one error in relating the ordinal and cardinal numbers during this second dramatization. As the children are dismissed, Tanya laments, "I never got a turn." Becky decides to repeat this experience the next day, adding an additional challenge by increasing the number of children in the play. She makes three more bus signs, with the numbers eight, nine, and ten.

The next day, when the children ask whether they can perform the "bus play" again, Becky is ready with her additional props and and her additions to the script. This time the children complete the drama without needing to make any corrections. Once the group of ten is in order, Becky asks a series of questions that will build up her students' understanding of ordinal numbers and other terms describing position:

> Who is third in line?
> What place is between fifth and seventh?
> Who is between Orin and Rosita?
> Who is next to Charlie?

It takes a while for the children to realize that both Kimi and José are next to Charlie. The children participate in this conversation with enthusiasm. Literature and drama have a way of sparking this kind of excitement.

Setting Contexts

Books don't have to be about mathematics in order to introduce mathematical ideas. Stories can provide contexts for mathematical investigations that motivate inquiry. An established context provides a mathematical task with authenticity. The familiar setting may also help the children feel confident and thus more able to negotiate mathematical meaning.

Corduroy's Pocket

This year Becky's class dearly loves the book *A Pocket for Corduroy* (Freeman 1978). In the story, Corduroy, a beloved stuffed bear belonging to a little girl named Lisa, has been left in the Laundromat. After she gets him back, Lisa sews a pocket on his overalls and puts an identification card inside it.

Becky uses her students' fascination with Corduroy as a hook for a problem that relates to subtraction:

> Corduroy has 6 stones in his pocket.
> He takes out 2 stones.
> How many stones does Corduroy have left in his pocket?

As the children tackle this problem, they refer often to the poster on which it is presented or ask each other, "How many stones does Corduroy have?" Once they have established the six original stones firmly in their mind, they model the information given in the problem, using actual stones, drawings of stones, cubes, or their fingers. Since this problem has only one correct answer, the focus is on the methods by which they arrive at their solutions. Early finishers are given the same problem to solve with different numbers of stones.

Once the children are familiar with the setting, Becky opens up the problem so that it has a number of answers:

> Corduroy has 5 stones in his pocket.
> He takes some stones out of his pocket.
> How many stones are left in Corduroy's pocket?

Even though it is late in the year, the children are perplexed at first. Becky encourages them to act out the story by placing five objects in their pocket. She then asks, "How many stones could Corduroy take out?," to help them get started. Two of their solutions are shown in Figures 6.9 and 6.10.

Over the next few weeks the children explore a variety of "pocket problems." One Monday morning Lisa comes to school with a tiny pouch. One of her teeth fell out over the weekend, and she has placed it in the pouch "for safe keeping" and has brought it to school to show everyone. She also brings in a math problem she has created (see Figure 6.11)!

FIGURE 6.9 A solution to the Corduroy's pocket problem

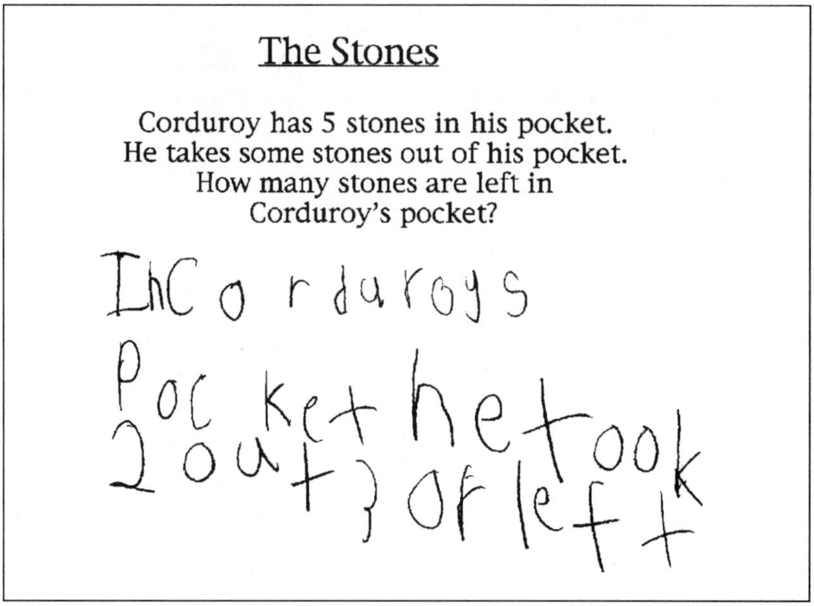

The Stones

Corduroy has 5 stones in his pocket.
He takes some stones out of his pocket.
How many stones are left in
Corduroy's pocket?

In Corduroys
Pocket he took
2 out? or left

FIGURE 6.10   Another solution to the Corduroy's pocket problem

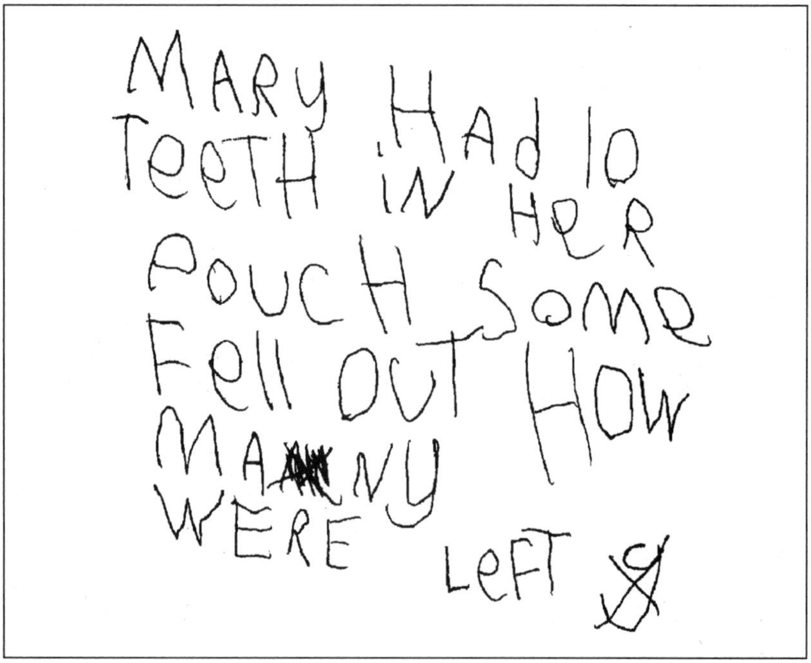

MARY HAD 10
TeeTH iN HeR
PoUCH Some
Fell oUT HoW
MANY
WERE LeFT

FIGURE 6.11   Lisa's teeth-in-a-pouch problem

Careful Use

Enthusiasm for using literature in the mathematics classroom surfaced in the early nineties and continues today. (Resource books that provide ideas for using specific books to teach mathematics are listed in Appendix A.) There are many wonderful children's books that lend themselves to mathematical investigations (twenty-five favorites for teaching mathematics in kindergarten are listed in Appendix B).

While children's literature has a wonderful place in the teaching of mathematics, we need to be careful about how we use it. As teachers we need to ask ourselves, *What are the best ways to use literature to promote mathematical thinking?* Here are some things to remember:

- It is important not to plunge into mathematical explorations before children have thoroughly identifed with the story. A book should be read several times to enable children to get to know it well.
- Young children learn mathematics best from the physical manipulation of objects. Reading a book cannot replace concrete models that can be moved and organized in order to construct mathematical ideas.
- It is important that the children, not us, do the mathematical work. While modeling is important, it is the children who need to develop the skills. While they need us to read the story to them, they should not rely on us for their mathematical thinking.
- It is important to build on the books we read to our students by having them retell the story, dramatize the story, create similar stories, make their own counting book, or model the action in a story with counters while they listen. Through these activities, the children are better able to make the literature and the mathematics their own.
- While big books are easier to read to a whole class, we should not avoid reading regular-size books in whole-group settings. Children will return to these books often, interacting with them individually or in small groups.
- We shouldn't overuse children's literature to teach

mathematics. Although children like a certain amount of repetition, they need variety as well.

- Not all books about mathematics are good examples of literature or contain thoughtful illustrations. If good literature is not available, it is better to use another teaching strategy.
- Sometimes books should be read just for fun.

Representing Mathematical Ideas

How do we, as adults, represent mathematical ideas? Most of us say or write numbers several times a day. And we probably use many other forms of representation during the course of a week, month, or year of which we are less aware. We may gesture to indicate that something is very small or use our fingers to count how many people are coming to dinner. When we are giving directions or planning a project, we may make maps, diagrams, and pictures to represent relationships of position, number, and size. These drawings are usually not standard representations but ones that are personally meaningful in a particular situation. Over time, we may create notations or symbols for physical objects and begin to use these representations consistently.

Traditionally, mathematics education has focused on the ability to use and interpret standard representations. In elementary school the focus has been on learning how to read and record numbers, write number sentences, and read information provided in expertly designed tables and graphs. While such skills are important to our culture, they are only one aspect of mathematical representation. To support the growth of mathematical ideas, children must also have opportunities to create their own ways to depict those ideas. Representation then becomes a way to construct or reconstruct knowledge, another step in the sense-making process (Hiebert et al. 1997).

Many teachers rely on worksheets or textbook exercises to gather evidence of children's learning, because these tangible, pencil-and-paper products often satisfy parents' and school officials' need to know that traditional learning goals are being met. Kindergarten teachers often feel pushed into providing work like this in order to meet the perceived expectations of first-grade teachers. In many classrooms this is the only type of representational work that is recognized. However, this is a very limited view of how children can represent mathematical ideas. It may also limit children's mathematical thinking and reasoning.

When representations are properly encouraged, they emerge as children interact with one another, with materials, and with a variety of settings. Representations may involve creating a physical model, dramatizing a situation, putting marks and drawings on paper, and recording numbers and words. Opportunities for kindergarten children to generate these representations should be a vital component of mathematical teaching and learning.

Collecting Data

Data collection is an excellent vehicle by which children can generate their own representations. Becky wants her students to conduct surveys and to create their own methods for keeping track of responses. She wants them to think about how to organize the collected data in a useful manner, one that communicates effectively and allows conclusions to be drawn easily. When young children first begin to conduct surveys, they are not necessarily concerned with these issues. Rather, they are excited about their questions and interested in interacting with classmates socially as they collect their data. After a while, however, their representations become more meaningful.

Some teachers set up their data collection assignments so there is no opportunity for critical thinking. They provide the survey question and a class list and tell the children to ask everyone the question and write yes or no after each name. This is a rote process; the children have no chance to invent their own questions and recording techniques. Invention arises from necessity. Once children understand that they need to create a system to record their data and keep track of whom they ask, they will begin to find ways to do so. Until then, the methods have no meaning.

Figures 7.1–7.4 are surveys conducted by Becky's students. The children choose their own question, which Becky writes at the top of their paper so that there will be more time for mathematics. Later in the year, however, the children record their own questions. Most of the questions posed can be answered yes or no. As you can see, the ways in which the children represent the results vary.

Rory (Figure 7.1) asks, "Do you like to play with blocks?" He randomly puts this question to nine of his classmates and has them sign his sheet. There is no representation indicating whether or not they like to play with blocks. Mei (Figure 7.2) asks, "Do you like to go to music?" She has the children who respond to her question record their names, along with a yes or a no. Tali (Figure 7.3) asks, "Do you like to go on a hike?" She sets up no and yes columns and shows children where to sign their names based on their responses. Jamal (Figure 7.4) asks, "What do you like to eat?" This question solicits categorical rather than numerical data, so it is more difficult to communicate the responses. Jamal writes the names of the respondents and their answers. A seasoned reader of invented spelling can learn that Ezra's favorite food is macaroni and cheese, that Becky and Jamal like clementines, that Charlie likes fried rice and hot peppers, that Mario likes pizza, and that Mei likes spaghetti. This is an incredible amount of writing for a young child. When Jamal gets to this point he says, "That's as much people as I can write down." Although exhausted, Jamal has asked a question that he finds interesting, one that would not have been possible with a prescribed yes-no format.

When children are allowed to follow their own interests, they are more motivated to represent their work, even if doing so is difficult. Over time, children create representations that are better organized and more efficient. What's more, their techniques are meaningful, because they have initiated them themselves. By encouraging children to share their techniques with their classmates, teachers can guide other children to identify potential

FIGURE 7.1   Rory's survey

FIGURE 7.2   Mei's survey

tools and strategies. These children can then try out the techniques and make them their own.

Making Maps

While data collection is now more common in kindergarten classrooms, map making is not. In December, a week before winter break, Becky decides to try something new. She knows that during this time of year the children need to be quite active in order to be engaged, so she plans a treasure hunt. She sets the stage for the activity by reading *The Secret Birthday Message*, by Eric Carle (1972). Three children have had birthdays the previous week, so there have been many conversations about birthdays. Also, the children are familiar with the author and fond of his books.

The story begins with a secret message that Tim receives the night before his birthday, a series of directions for him to follow in order to find his birthday gift. The directions contain words

FIGURE 7.3 Tali's survey

and geometric figures. As Becky reads the secret message to the children, she encourages them to guess the meaning of each shape. Tim follows the directions and finds a puppy. At the end of the story, Carle provides a map of Tim's journey. The map includes more realistic pictures of the places represented in the message by geometric shapes, with arrows leading from one place to another. After Becky finishes reading the book, she reviews the map and asks the children to retell the story. Then it's time for recess.

During recess, while a colleague watches her students, Becky hides clues around the room, and then posts a letter on the outside of the classroom door:

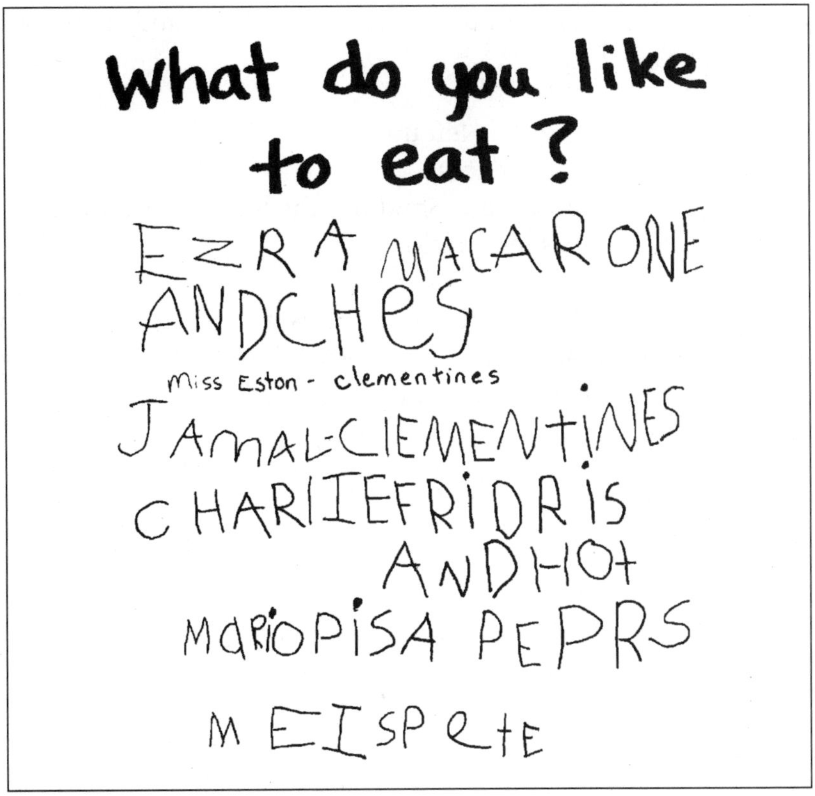

FIGURE 7.4 Jamal's survey

Dear Friends in Room 103,

If you work as a team and follow each clue,
I have left a treat for you.

Love,
Guess Who?

Attached to the letter is an envelope labeled *Clue #1*. Then Becky closes the classroom door and goes outside to call the children in from recess.

The children who have walked ahead of Becky come rushing back. "Miss Eston, Miss Eston, something is wrong. There is a big piece of paper on our door and the door is closed!" Becky asks everyone to hang up his or her coat in the hallway and then gather around the door. Once they are all assembled, Becky reads the letter. The children begin to whisper and then some speak out.

EZRA: I think the elves left this.
HALEY: Maybe it was Santa.
KIMI: Maybe it was Mrs. Smithlin [the teacher next door].
SAMMY: What does the envelope say?

When the children realize there is a clue, they insist that Becky read it immediately. Becky opens the envelope and shows the children the clue as she reads.

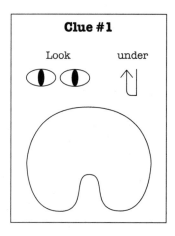

BECKY: WHAT DO YOU THINK THIS MEANS?
JAMAL: I think they want us to look under the telephone. [*All of the children dash into the classroom and the first one to reach the telephone picks up the receiver . . . but no clue is found.*]
SETH: I think it is the bean table. [*He and a few other children head to the middle of the classroom and check out the bean table.*]
RORY: It's not here.
ANA: Wait, it said "under." [*Rory, Ana, and Seth dive under the table.*]
SETH: I found it!
EVERYONE: Open it! Open it!
BECKY: LET'S SEE WHAT THIS CLUE SAYS. [*She reads the clue and*

*small groups of children scatter off in different
directions.*]

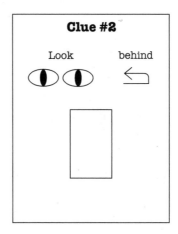

LISA: It's a rectangle, right?

CHARLIE: No, it's a door.

KAITLIN: It could be a table.

ALLISON: [*Emerging from the dramatic play area*] I found it. It
was taped behind the door of the refrigerator.

EVERYONE: Read it! Read it! [*Becky reads the clue.*]

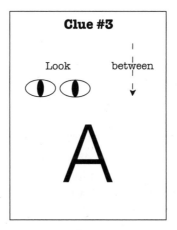

ORIN: It's an A.

NICOLE: Where is there an A in our classroom?

ANA: There's lots on the walls.

CHARLIE: This is too hard.

BECKY: LOOK AROUND AND SEE IF YOU GET ANY IDEAS.

TANYA: It's like the side of the easels. [*The children scatter to the easels in the room, and the final clue is found and read.*]

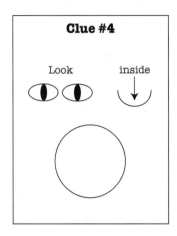

MEI: It could be the round table.

JOSÉ: No. You can't look inside there.

RORY: The window in the door.

TALI: You can't get inside there, either.

HALEY: What about a bucket?

The children rush to the math/science area to check the buckets in which unit blocks are stored. Inside one of them, the children find a bag of small chocolate candies.

After the candy has been shared and eaten, the children gather in the meeting area. They are eager to talk about their adventure; it is obvious that the activity has excited them. They read the clues again, the visual icons jogging their memory of each one, as they retell the story of their treasure hunt. When one of the children says, "This is just like the birthday story," Becky reminds them of the map at the end of the book. She shows them the page again, in case some children have forgotten it, and asks them to make a map of their treasure hunt.

The children must find their own way to depict what they have done. While making their drawings, the children review the order of the clues, asking questions like *What did we do second?*

When there is disagreement, they return to the clues, which have been posted in the meeting area. Some children represent the action of one clue, and then go back to read the next clue. Others walk through the entire clue sequence before they make their drawings. Still others remain seated, but follow the path with their eyes.

As they complete their work, Becky has them retell the story of the hunt as shown in their drawings. The majority of the drawings are linear representations of the five locations: classroom door, table, refrigerator door, easel, and bucket (see the example in Figure 7.5). Lines or arrows often connect the items, as in the map in the book. A few children leave out one of the locations or get one or two in the wrong order. However, most of the drawings are accurate.

A few of the children try to show the configuration of the room. These nonlinear representations are enclosed in rectangles to show the perimeter of the classroom and often provide additional details. Sammy's map, shown in Figure 7.6, is fairly typical. Note the numbers that indicate the clues and the Xs that show the people.

Two of the children make unique representations. Kaitlin uses numbers to stand for the order of the clues (see Figure 7.7). Rosita tries to record the positional prepositions as well (see

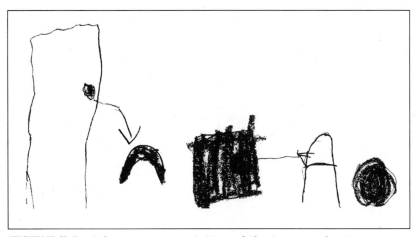

FIGURE 7.5   A linear representation of the treasure hunt

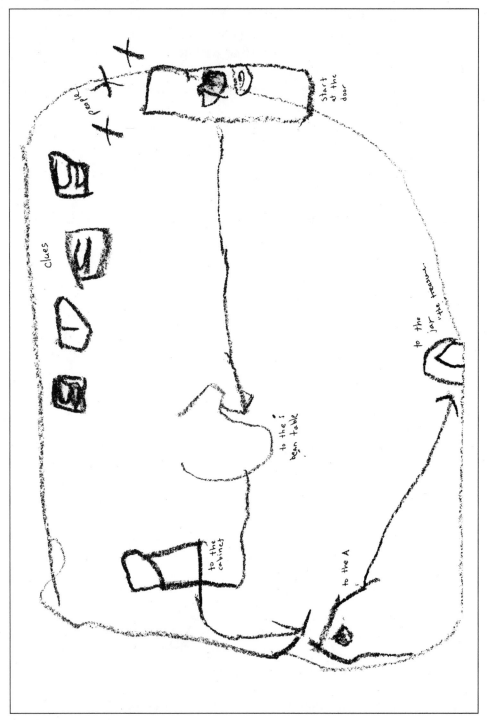

FIGURE 7.6 Sammy's map, showing the configuration of the room

FIGURE 7.7   Kaitlin's numbered representation of the treasure hunt

Figure 7.8). When asked why she did not include the final step, Rosita replies, "I'm too tired." As so often is the case at this age, completeness is not necessarily a criteria for being finished.

When she designed this treasure hunt, Becky wanted the children to have to focus on the meaning of the prepositions she used in the clues as well as on two-dimensional representations of three-dimensional objects. She picked a somewhat unique shape for the first clue, because she wanted the children to be able to decipher it easily. For the remaining clues, she purposely chose shapes that were more common in the classroom and thus more challenging. The ambiguity allowed the children to look in a variety of places and to discuss the numerous possibilities. It also helped them link particular geometric shapes with a variety of objects.

As the children worked on representing their hunt, they used ordinal terms and made a meaningful map. While it is not common for kindergarten children to engage in work like this, they

FIGURE 7.8   Rosita's representation includes prepositions

are clearly capable of doing so successfully. It is important for even young children to learn that they are able to represent complex ideas and actions.

Ultimately, Becky wants children to generalize what they learn and apply it to new situations, to make connections among their ideas. Sometimes they do so rather quickly. For example, when Haley brought in the Mystery Box (in which she had placed some coins) the next day, she offered these three clues:

They are shiny.

They are from another country.

They are this big.

This was the first time anyone had used a drawing in the Mystery Box clues. When Becky asked Haley about her third clue, Haley replied, "I thought of it from yesterday." Mapping the treasure hunt caused Haley to realize that making drawings of shapes is a useful way to communicate information. She was able to apply this representational tool to a new setting.

Three months later, Becky plans another treasure hunt for her class. She plants the first clue in a book she pretends she is going to read in the meeting area. As she picks up the book and opens it, the clue falls to the floor. Becky says, "Hmm, what is this? It looks like a clue." Sammy immediately jumps up and declares, "Oh boy, we're going to have another treasure hunt!" The children are very excited as they discover the clues behind the computer, under the globe, between the oversize dice, and inside the trash barrel.

Once again Becky asks the children to represent their journeys. Although they have done no additional map making in the intervening time, their ability to draw has clearly progressed. Many more of them show the configuration of the room rather than present the clues in a row across the paper. Details have increased and more use numbers to show the order of the clues. While Rory's representation (Figure 7.9) shows the book where the first clue is found, his numbers begin with the first designated place, the computer. Lisa begins to number at the book (see Figure 7.10). As she often does, Becky notes the children's articulation of the process directly on their maps and marvels at their unique abilities for creating representations.

Solving Story Problems

Long before they have received formal instruction in arithmetic, young children can solve a variety of story problems (involving multiplication and division as well as addition and subtraction) by modeling the actions and relationships described. Including such problems in the kindergarten curriculum gives children the opportunity to learn the importance of modeling as a problem-solving strategy. It also allows young children to build a strong, intuitive understanding of story-problem actions that can be associated later with more formal representations. Finally, it presents mathematics as the act of making sense out of information in order to solve problems.

Then to the dice

Then I got to the joke.

Then to the trash can

I started from here. The computer.

FIGURE 7.9 Rory's representation of the second treasure hunt

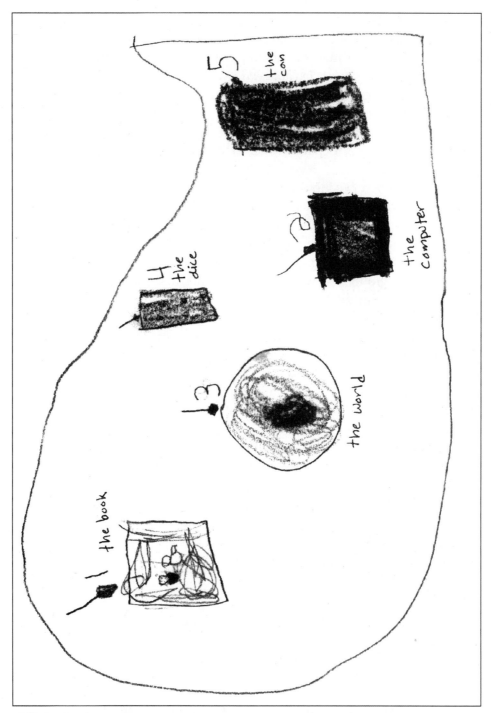

FIGURE 7.10 Lisa's representation of the second treasure hunt

To solve a particular story problem, children must connect that problem to a model of what the story is about. The model may be physical, pictorial, or mental. Consider the story problem *Maggie has 6 crayons. Lucinda has 4 crayons. Altogether, how many crayons do they have?* To create a model, children must reformulate the problem, focusing on its salient features. They will extract different amounts and types of data and construct a variety of representations, depending on their developmental levels and learning styles.

Some children need to dramatize the situation with real girls (perhaps referring to them as Maggie and Lucinda) and real crayons. Some can use pictures of both the girls and the crayons. Other children may be able to use counters for the crayons but still require pictures of two girls. In initial stages, most children represent each group of crayons separately and then count them all, following the suggested action in the story.

In the process of creating these representations, children may transform their understanding of the task. Meanings evolve and shift. Eventually, some children represent the six crayons and add the four crayons to that set, without needing to create two separate sets first. Over time, children develop a schema for joining two sets that can be generalized to all similar problems. The action is connected to a number sentence. Drawings or fingers are used instead of objects. Ultimately, a physical model is replaced with a mental one. At each stage in the process, a representation is involved that mediates the sense making (Meira 1995).

Becky admits that she sometimes underestimates young students' ability to solve complex story problems. It is amazing what young students can do. On the day after Becky's class went on a nature walk, she proposes this problem:

The Hike

There are 2 groups of children taking a hike.
There are 5 children in each group.
3 children stop to tie their shoes.
How many children keep walking?

Becky posts the problem on the math easel in the meeting area. She doesn't expect the children to be able to read the problem on their own but offers it in print for two reasons: she wants to expose them to written language, and she wants them to be able to refer to the problem later if they wish.

Becky reads the problem through once. Then she reads it many more times with the children joining in, much in the spirit of shared reading. Next, Becky asks the children to retell the problem in their own words. (Remember, they are retelling the story at this point, not sharing solutions or strategies.) By hearing and retelling the story, they begin to get invested in the problem and find ways to recall the vital information.

For children who recognize that "two groups of five" is easily represented with fingers, this problem is more accessible. Before the children even discuss the problem, a couple of them are already modeling it. Nicole quickly looks at her fingers and stretches out all ten of them as Becky first reads the problem. During subsequent readings, Nicole tucks seven fingers into her fists, showing three fingers pointing out. She counts the tucked fingers and under her breath says, "Seven."

Nicole knows immediately that she can use her ten fingers to represent the two groups of five children. She explains, "I know that five and five is ten, so I put out ten fingers." Then she clearly represents the action of the hikers on her fingers: "These are the ones that stopped. The others keep going." The action of folding in all of the fingers but three is Nicole's way of differentiating the hikers that stopped from those that kept walking. Nicole does not know that seven hikers continue walking, however, until she counts her remaining fingers.

Most children need to use materials. As it is March, the children have solved many simpler story problems. They know that manipulatives like Unifix cubes, teddy bear counters, or stones are always available. It is up to the children to decide whether they want to use physical materials and if so, which ones. They also know that they can work together to dramatize the problem, draw pictures, write words, and use numbers in any way that makes sense.

The children work diligently. Tanya tries to represent the problem with Unifix cubes. She takes out five cubes and places them on the table. Next she moves three of them to one side and says her answer is two. Becky asks Tanya to retell the story. Tanya does so and then quickly puts a second group of five cubes on the table. This time she takes away three cubes from each row of five and says the answer is four. She then looks at the pile of six cubes and says, "No, that's supposed to be three."

"What's supposed to be three?" asks Becky.

"Only three kids stop," Tanya explains. Then she puts all ten cubes back on the table (now placed in one row) and takes away three cubes without counting. She counts the remaining cubes and says, "Now I know the answer is seven."

Tanya constructs a model that matches the problem and then manipulates it to show the action of the story. While she struggles somewhat with how to represent the story, her familiarity with it allows her to check her work, note her error, and amend her model and solution.

The children know that Becky expects them to try to record their work in some way. Although Nicole has used her fingers to represent the story, she doesn't trace them onto her paper. Instead, she shows the answer by recording the symbol for seven, albeit reversed, and attempts to write the word *seven*. (See Figure 7.11.)

Mei finds her solution by drawing five children in a line across her page. Then she draws five more people. At this point,

The Hike

There are 2 groups of children taking a hike.
There are 5 children in each group.
3 children stop to tie their shoes.
How many children keep walking?

FIGURE 7.11 Nicole's solution

she erases three of them and redraws them to show a second group, the group that stopped. Mei writes 7 next to the story to show her answer. (See Figure 7.12.) For Mei, drawing people is perhaps more concrete than using counters to represent people.

Ezra uses Unifix cubes. He counts two groups of five cubes and puts them together in a line. He then sets three cubes aside. He records his process on paper, carefully matching the colors of his ten cubes. He takes great pains to match the colors exactly, apparently believing that it is an important part of the process. He then draws a vertical line after the third cube to show that three children stopped to tie their shoes. He also writes 7. (See Figure 7.13.)

Sammy records *7 PEPL.* Because Becky has not seen Sammy arrive at his answer, she wants to make sure that he understands the problem. She asks him to show her more about his thinking. Sammy returns later with a drawing on his paper (see Figure 7.14).

FIGURE 7.12 Mei's solution

The Hike

There are 2 groups of children taking a hike.

There are 5 children in each group.

3 children stop to tie their shoes.

How many children keep walking?

FIGURE 7.13 Ezra's solution

The Hike

There are 2 groups of children taking a hike.

There are 5 children in each group.

3 children stop to tie their shoes.

How many children keep walking?

FIGURE 7.14 Sammy's solution

The drawing shows a mountain with five Xs on each side. "These are the hikers," he says. "These [pointing to the three that are scribbled over] are the ones that stopped walking. That makes seven." Clearly, he understands the problem.

Ben is able to represent the problem mentally and arrive at the correct answer. His recording shows all ten hikers. He uses labels to indicate the action in the problem, writing *go* above the first seven figures and *stop* above the remaining three. (See Figure 7.15.)

About two thirds of the children solve the problem correctly. However, many of the others are able to construct a partial

FIGURE 7.15 Ben's solution

understanding of the situation. Kaitlin's drawing (Figure 7.16) is typical. It shows only one group of five children, three of whom stop while two go on.

This is the first time the students have solved this type of problem and Becky is pleased with the results. Almost all the children are able to form representations that are at least partially correct, and most of them arrive at correct solutions. No one is frustrated by the work, and many children present clever recordings.

The Hike

There are 2 groups of children taking a hike.
There are 5 children in each group.
3 children stop to tie their shoes.
How many children keep walking?

FIGURE 7.16   Kaitlin's solution

Using Standard Notation

Children are able to recognize symbols for numbers long before they are able to write them. Young children lack the fine motor skills and eye-hand coordination necessary to write numerals and letters easily. Nevertheless, most first-grade teachers expect children to be able to record numbers. So, while most of Becky's attention is spent on developing an understanding of number relationships and what they mean, she also deals with recording numbers.

Many children develop the ability to write the numerals for one through ten in preschool or at home. Others need systematic procedures to guide them. Rhymes like *Down and over, and down some more, that's the way to make a four* may be helpful to some children. Most just need practice. Whenever the practice can be embedded in activities, it is more meaningful.

To give her students meaningful practice, Becky has them play a game called Dice Race. She gives them recording sheets with segmented columns above each of the numbers one through six. They roll dice and record the numbers shown in the appropriate columns, starting with the bottom segment. The first number on each player's sheet to be completely filled in is the "winner" of that player's game. (See the example in Figure 7.17.) The children enjoy the game and play it frequently. When a game is completed Becky reviews the record sheet with the player, asking questions like *How many times did you roll a two?* She may also ask *Do you see anything different about this three?* to help children recognize numerals that are not written correctly.

Children include numbers in representations as they become familiar with the written symbols. At this early age, however, children may still forget the symbols for certain numbers, reverse their formation, or confuse a six and a nine or a five and a two. Over time, most of these errors will lessen. Becky tries not to pay too much attention to errors in the midst of representations that have required a great deal of work. Hearing *The six is wrong* can be very deflating to a child who has just worked arduously to record his or her work. Besides, a comment like this places the emphasis on handwriting, not on mathematical thinking.

As children investigate story problems, Becky introduces

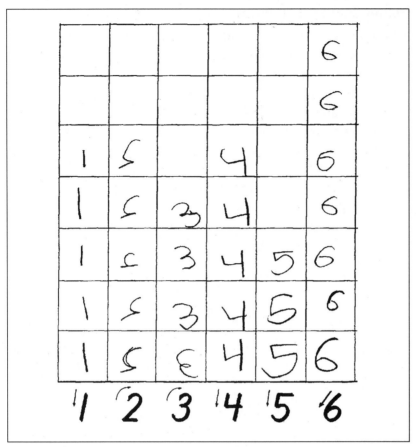

FIGURE 7.17   A Dice Race recording sheet

the use of number sentences to represent the action of the story. It will be a couple of years before children master addition and subtraction notation, but early exposure to these recording techniques is valuable. During a class meeting, Becky may write *4 + 2 = 6* as a student says, "I added two more to the four and I got six." She then explains that this is another way to represent what was said.

Some children will invent their own notation, just as they invent other forms of representation. One day, Rosita is working on her own in the art center. When she finishes, she proudly shows her paper to Becky (see Figure 7.18) and says, "I've been making additions." When Becky asks her what the circles mean, Rosita explains that she put the circle around the two so that it

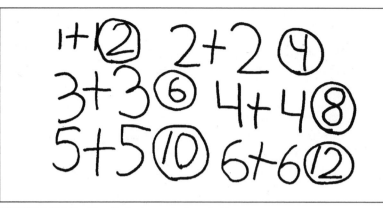

FIGURE 7.18   Rosita's invented notation

wouldn't look like twelve. Rosita has recognized the need for a symbol between the addends and the sum. After congratulating Rosita on her technique, Becky says, "Let me show you the symbol other people use." This way, Rosita does not feel that she is being corrected or that her work is being slighted. Instead, her technique is linked to one that others use and the equal sign becomes meaningful.

Making Connections

The representation of mathematical ideas requires children to translate those ideas into new forms. When ideas are understood, children are able to represent them in a variety of ways and make connections among those representations. Children need to connect real-life contexts, manipulatives, pictures, written symbols, and verbal symbols. For example, we expect children to recognize sevens in several forms. Children should make links among a group of seven counters; a picture of seven objects; the symbol 7; the word *seven*; and real-life questions like *How many days are there in a week?* Further, they need to make connections within these modes of representation (Lesh 1979). For example, children should be able to translate a pattern made with red and blue tiles to one made with green and yellow ones.

Thinking about a variety of ways to represent ideas can help guide our instructional decisions. When designing lessons, we need to remind ourselves to plan specific opportunities for children to make connections within and among various forms of representation. Such connections solidify mathematical ideas and support further growth. When assessing our students' progress and the effectiveness of our curriculum, we should ask such questions as:

- Which representational forms does the child seem to prefer?
- Is there a representational form that the child rarely uses?
- Has the child built connections among and within representational forms for concepts of number? shape? pattern?
- For which concepts are only some forms of representation understood?

By paying attention to questions like this, we can begin to delineate a child's ability to represent mathematical ideas, noting changes over time. Young children are very capable, and they (and we) can learn much from their representational work.

8

Assessing Mathematical Understanding

The word *assess* derives from a Latin root (*as* + *sidere*) meaning *to sit down beside*. Teachers have heard much about assessment in the past few years, in terms both of new assessment strategies and of a heightened concern with accountability. Kindergarten teachers have been "sitting down beside" their students for many years. Most early-childhood teachers intuitively monitor the needs and abilities of their students from the time they enter the classroom each morning. They observe their students' thinking, albeit informally, while circulating among them and assisting them throughout the day. The challenge is how best to use and document this informal system of gathering information to guide instructional choices in mathematics.

Ideally, assessment is a means that allows us to meet instructional goals. Good assessment practices help us make more informed pedagogical decisions, document student growth, and communicate with our students, their parents, and others. Through such practices we constantly hone our abilities to make sound judgments about student performance. Simultaneously, we refine our visions of what our students know and what we think they need to know.

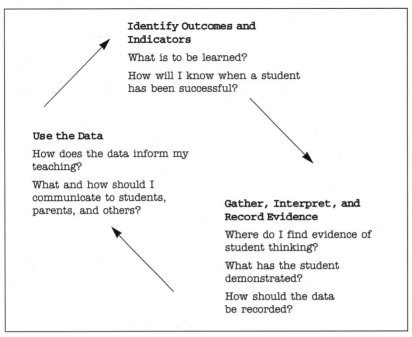

FIGURE 8.1   A model of the assessment cycle (Moon and Schulman 1995, p. 11)

Assessment begins when we identify outcomes, or learning goals, that determine the instructional agenda in our classrooms. We then think about what a student would do to demonstrate that she or he has attained these goals. (Such behavior is often referred to as a performance indicator or standard.) Next, we collect evidence that documents student understanding, organize these data and, most important, interpret them using our professional knowledge of children and mathematics. Finally, these interpretations inform our instructional decisions and support our communication with others about what has been learned. This assessment cycle is depicted graphically in Figure 8.1.

Identifying Outcomes and Indicators

Chapter 3 illustrates how to define curricular goals by identifying big ideas and delineating them using a content map. Through this strategy, Becky identifies the outcomes she wants her students to achieve. Now, she needs to identify the behavior that indicates a child has achieved those outcomes. For example, posing questions is one of four key processes in a data investigation. What kinds of behavior does Becky want to foster in her students in terms of posing questions? After some deliberation, she decides she wants students to:

- Display a natural curiosity and ask questions frequently.
- Ask many types of questions, not just those that can be answered yes or no.
- Display divergent thinking by asking a variety of questions about the same situation.
- Re-form their questions based on the answers they receive in order to clarify data.
- Identify follow-up questions in order to probe more deeply.

Identifying these performance indicators demonstrated by good problem posers helps Becky create learning opportunities that nurture their development. It also initiates the assessment process: by identifying the desired behavior, she has defined the type of evidence she should collect. This evidence will in turn inform Becky's instructional decisions. She has embarked on a seamless loop of curriculum, instruction, and assessment.

Gathering, Interpreting, and Recording Evidence

Kidwatching, a term coined by educator Yetta Goodman, is one of Becky's favorite activities. As she observes a child, she thinks about what she sees and what it tells her about that child's current understanding of mathematics. At the same time, she thinks about this level of understanding in terms of the mathematical learning path she expects the child to follow. In this way, her observations inform her instructional decisions.

Since Becky observes many children, many times, every day, she makes some observations and decisions of which she is totally unaware. On the other hand, she does document some of what she notices. This allows her to review data over time and to make sure that evidence for reflective decision making really exists. It is difficult to juggle all of this information, and she has worked hard to create ways to manage assessment data more easily.

Informal Observations and Anecdotal Records

In order to use her observations, Becky needs to write them down and then organize her records. She first tried using Post-it notes or index cards but found them too cumbersome. They often got lost in the shuffle of papers at the end of the day.

Next she tried using monthly calendar grids (see Figure 8.2). She created one sheet for each student, alphabetized the sheets by first name, and placed them on her clipboard. At any given moment she could record notes about a child's learning style, attitude, socialization, acclamation, and performance. This worked much better, and Becky managed her anecdotal records this way for several years.

One of the most beneficial aspects about the calendar grids was that she could quickly identify the children about whom she had gathered lots of information and those about whom she had not. These inconsistencies are important; they are never intentional but are often very telling. Realizing that she didn't record as much information about her quieter students helped Becky remember to focus on all children and their differing learning styles.

After a few years of using this system, Becky noticed that while she took notes diligently at the beginning of each year, by midyear she rarely wrote on these sheets. Perhaps this change had to do with the increased pace of the year or with knowing her students better. She wondered, though, if this style of record keeping was too restrictive or too cumbersome for her to maintain. She decided to try a different approach to gathering and organizing her observations.

Together with a colleague, Becky created a form that she could use when observing any activity at any time (see Figure 8.3). The form prompts her to record the date and the focus of the activity as well as the student's name. The relatively large space in which to write allows her to record more information when she needs to do so. Becky leaves three clipboards filled with these forms around the room so that she can reach one wherever

Name Date

Monday	Tuesday	Wednesday	Thursday	Friday

FIGURE 8.2 A monthly calendar grid for anecdotal record keeping

```
┌─────────────────────────────────────────────────────────────┐
│                                                               │
│  Student: _____  Date: _____    │
│  Activity / Focus: _____ │
│  Observations / Comments:                                     │
│                                                               │
│                                                               │
│                                                               │
│                                                               │
│                                                               │
│                                                               │
│                                                               │
│  Student: _____  Date: _____    │
│  Activity / Focus: _____ │
│  Observations / Comments:                                     │
│                                                               │
│                                                               │
│                                                               │
│                                                               │
│                                                               │
│                                                               │
│                                                               │
│  Student: _____  Date: _____    │
│  Activity / Focus: _____ │
│  Observations / Comments:                                     │
│                                                               │
└─────────────────────────────────────────────────────────────┘
```

FIGURE 8.3   A blank form for recording observations

she and the children may be working. She makes a note when she sees or hears something she wants to remember. She indicates her own comments to the children by preceding them with a circled T (see Figure 8.4).

At the end of each week, Becky collects these sheets, cuts them apart or photocopies them if they contain notes about more than one student, and rereads them before placing them

Student: __Nicole__   Date: __4·8·98__

Activity / Focus: __Self Initiated Survey__

Observations / Comments:

"Is everyone on my list?"

Ⓣ "How can you tell?"

"Count. But I want to know who I have. I have 18, but I can't read the names."

Ⓣ "What else can you do?"

"I guess I could check the letters.

N. went over to the name graph and worked for a while. Later she came to me with her sheet. She had added more names and a code for the kids absent.

Student: __Mario__   Date: __4·8·98__

Activity / Focus: __How many in the class representation__

Observations / Comments:

Mario had worked for a long time on his drawing. When I asked him about it, he made no response. This seems to be a common occurrence. Why?

Student: __Nicole__   Date: __4·9·98__

Activity / Focus: __Block Grab - Pattern Blocks__

Observations / Comments:

Nicole's recording sheet showed Y3 B2 G4. When I asked her about this she told me it was a code: Y- yellow B- blue G- green.

"It's just like I did for the snack problem. Remember?

R- raisin G- carrot

FIGURE 8.4 A filled-in observation form

in the respective student's folder. This way of managing her observations has worked well for her. Since she is able to continue using it throughout the year, she can compare her notes over time.

Becky also records simple observations of several students working on the same activity, often writing only a few key words and adding more detail later. For example, one day the children are playing Collect 15 Together (Kliman et al. 1998, p. 17). In pairs, they take turns rolling a die and picking up that number of counters. They keep rolling and collecting counters until they have at least fifteen counters. The children have already played a simpler version of this game in which they collected only ten counters. They are familiar with the activity and yet challenged by the greater number.

Becky observes Luke and Rosita at play. Luke identifies the last bear he touches as fifteen. Rosita reminds him that this means that together the entire set is a quantity of fifteen. Is Luke sure of this? By recording the notes shown in Figure 8.5, Becky reminds herself to check in with Luke another day about this important concept.

Becky also takes notes about other students playing this same game (see Figure 8.6). Reviewing these notes later, Becky realizes that she often records very different observations about the same activity. This variety helps her understand better the different learning issues and learning styles among her students. It also deepens her understanding of teaching mathematics at

---

Student: ___Luke and Rosita___   *Date:* ___2·11·98___
Activity / Focus: ___Collect 15___
Observations / Comments:

   L - successfully counts set of bears. "This is 15." Hold up
      last bear and shows R.

   R - Places hands on all of the bears. "No, this is 15."

   L - Yeah, I guess so.

FIGURE 8.5 Becky's notes on Luke and Rosita's game of Collect 15

Student: ___Kimi and Seth___ Date: _2·11·98_

Activity / Focus: ___Collect 15___

Observations / Comments:

S - Counts 13. "Now we only have to do 14, 15.

K rolls a 1.

S - "One, that will work."

S - seems easily distracted and keeps the piles of chips rolled separate.

Student: ___Charlie and Orin___ Date: ___2·11·98___

Activity / Focus: ___Collect 15___

Observations / Comments:

C touches each block to count and gets 8. Rolls die and puts out 3 more. Recounts entire group and gets 12. Seems to count randomly.

O - Watches C count. "I get 11."

C recounts and gets 11.

Does C have a technique for keeping track?

Student: ___Katlin and Nicole___ Date: _2·11·98_

Activity / Focus: ___Collect 15___

Observations / Comments:

K - confident. Asked to play again. Suggested playing for a "bigger number."

N - Wanted to discuss rules. When she had 14 and rolled a 3, she didn't think that worked. "Too many. Let's roll until we get a 1."

FIGURE 8.6   More notes on Collect 15

this level. It is not, however, part of a systematic or objective plan. By documenting her observations for several years, she has come to trust her intuition. She does not always have to be methodical.

At times, Becky ties her observations to identified goals in a unit. During a unit on patterns, for example, she wants to make sure that she gathers data about several pattern-related abilities. By listing them on one recording form (see Figure 8.7), Becky is better able to keep focused. For a couple of days, or perhaps a week, her mathematical anecdotal records will be centered on these listed items.

At other times, Becky writes something down because it sparks her curiosity, even though she may not know at the time if or why it is important. Later she thinks about what she has noted and how it might help her learn about the particular children involved and about teaching and learning in general. For example, Becky was so taken by a conversation she overheard while her students were waiting for the bus that when the buses left she quickly returned to her room and wrote it down.

TALI: How old are you?
KIMI: I don't know.
TALI: You don't know how old you are?
KIMI: No.
TALI: I'm six. Are you?
KIMI: No, my mom says I'm not six yet.
TALI: Then you're five.
KIMI: No, I'm not five anymore, but I'm not six either.
TALI: If you're not six, then you are five.
KIMI: No.
LISA: She can be five and a half.
KIMI: No, I'm not that either. But I know I'm not six yet. I don't know what I am.

Becky chuckled as she walked back from the bus. She thought about how often adults hold on to a younger age until the very last moment and then reluctantly say they are the next year older. Kimi, on the other hand, seems to have outgrown being five. Since she is not yet six, however, she is not sure what

Pattern Assessment

Name: _____   Date: _____

1. Can copy a pattern?   Yes   No
      Types of pattern copied:
      Comments/Observations: _____

2. Can construct a pattern?   Yes   No
      Types of pattern constructed:
      Comments/Observations: _____

3. Can extend a pattern?   Yes   No
      Types of patterns extended:
      Comments/Observations: _____

4. Can identify the unit of a
   repeated pattern?   Yes   No
      Types of units identified: _____
      Comments/Observations:

5. Can reconstruct a pattern after
   it has been broken apart?   Yes   No
      Comments/Observations: _____

FIGURE 8.7   Becky's pattern assessment recording form

she is. Rereading her transcription of this conversation triggered a series of questions for Becky:

- Does Kimi think that she was only five for a day? a week? a month?
- What does this say about the complexities of our number system?
- How do other children learn that there is continuity between the day you turn five and the day you turn six?
- Do older children recognize ages as continuous data?

Dialogues like this do not fit neatly on restricted forms, however. The final change that Becky has made to her recording system is that she now keeps blank paper on her clipboards as well, in order to capture these lengthier conversations.

It is often difficult for Becky to know just what and how much information to record. Does she need to record everything? There have been times when she felt as if she were frantically trying to do so. This is impossible, of course, so she has had to work out for herself how, when, and how much information to write on her anecdotal records. She reminds herself that they are to help, not hinder, her teaching and that they are never to interfere with her relationships with students.

Structured Observations

Most teachers have phrases they use or actions they take when they want their students' attention immediately. In Becky's classroom the children learn to stop everything they are doing and remain silent when they hear Becky say *Stop, look, and listen*. Becky realizes this is good advice with regard to her assessment practices as well. So she sometimes stops to take a closer look at students' developing skills.

While her daily anecdotal notes focus primarily on the children's thinking and the processes and language they use in their investigations, Becky's structured observations allow her to monitor more closely her students' mastery of important skills. They are a way for Becky to make sure that the children can accomplish what she thinks they can. They are also another way for her to document the growth of mathematical ideas over the course of the year.

This year Becky has added a new classroom activity, the Counting Jar. (She learned about this activity from Investigations in Number, Data and Space, *Collecting, Counting and Measuring* [Murray, Economopoulos, Kliman 1998].) Becky prepares for this activity by putting a number of objects inside a clear plastic container. One day she might use small blocks, another day she might use tiles, keys, or toy plastic dinosaurs. In the beginning of the year she puts between five and twelve objects in the jar, toward the end, between twenty and thirty objects. In pairs or alone, the children empty the jar and count the objects. Individually, they then represent that number on a Post-it note. They place their representation on a poster and then head off to make a set of that same number of things. Each child has a plastic plate with his or her name preprinted on it, on which to place the equivalent set. The plates help to contain the objects and are used to display the work on a table.

When all the children have had the opportunity to participate in the activity (usually over a period of two or three days), they count the contents of the jar as a class. Then a new set of objects is put in the jar, the new jar is introduced during a morning meeting, and the activity is repeated. Once the children understand the activity and are able to complete it accurately, Becky may ask them to make a set of objects one more or one less than the number in the jar. She may also let pairs of students take responsibility for filling the jar. Over time, Becky includes estimation in the process, holding up the jar and asking, *Do you think there are more or less than five objects in the jar? more than ten? more or less than in the jar we counted yesterday?*

This routine gives the students regular opportunities to count, to develop techniques that help them count more accurately, and to represent numbers. It also gives Becky many chances to observe her students' counting skills and understanding. With so many children doing this activity so many times, Becky needs a way to structure her observations.

Every time students perform the Counting Jar activity, Becky asks one or two children to perform the counting routine in her presence and notes his or her work on a task-specific recording form. Over time, Becky is able to compare the forms and document the growth of mathematical ideas and skills. Figures 8.8 and 8.9 are forms Becky completed as Haley performed the task in December and again in April.

_____Haley_____'s Counting Jar Assessments

Date: _12·12·97_   Number of Items in Jar: ___14___

□ Counting a Set of Objects:

    Randomly counts set

    (Removes or touches one item at a time)

    Other organizational strategies

    Double-checks work

☑ Uses correct sequence of number names

□ Recording Numerical Information:

    (Uses Pictures) makes tally marks.

    Uses Numbers (Note strategies for determining the number)
                  writes 41
    Uses words

    Other

□ Creating a New Set of a Given Size:

    Recalls target number No → Ⓣ Do you remember the number?
                                        "No"
    (Counts out a new set) Ⓣ How can you find out?
                             "I can count them. 14"
    Compares items in some way
    Double-Checks Ⓣ Is there another way you could find out?
                             "I don't know."

FIGURE 8.8 Haley's December counting jar assessment

_____Haley_____'s Counting Jar Assessments

Date: ___4.3.98___ Number of Items in Jar: ___17___

☐ Counting a Set of Objects:

    Randomly counts set

    ⟨Removes or touches one item at a time⟩

    Other organizational strategies

    Double-checks work

☑ Uses correct sequence of number names

☐ Recording Numerical Information:

    Uses Pictures

    ⟨Uses Numbers⟩ (Note strategies for determining the number)
         writes 17
    Uses words

    Other

☐ Creating a New Set of a Given Size:

    ⟨Recalls target number⟩

    ⟨Counts out a new set⟩

    Compares items in some way

    ⟨Double-Checks⟩

    "It's 17. I double-checked."

FIGURE 8.9 Haley's April counting jar assessment

Assessment Interviews

Becky and the other kindergarten teachers at her school also use an "assessment interview" focusing on number. The questions deal with four tasks: rote counting, number recognition, writing numerals, and counting sets of objects.

Twice a year (in late September or early October, as a baseline, and in February, just before parent conferences) Becky interviews each of her students. She often conducts the interview a third time, in May or June, with children about whom she is less sure.

First, Becky asks the student to predict how high she can count. Following the prediction, the student counts by rote. Becky then asks the child if she knows any other ways to count (in response, the child might count backward, skip count, or count in another language). If the child does not respond, Becky might prompt, *Can you count backward?*

Next, Becky gives the child a piece of paper with several numerals on it (see Figure 8.10). Becky and her colleagues developed this sheet based on what they know about assessment in literacy: showing a variety of letters to a child at once, rather than showing him individual letters on flash cards, gives him the opportunity to focus on the letters he knows, experience success, and gain confidence. The same is true when a child is asked to identify numerals. (The symbols for larger numbers are on the

---

Number Recognition - At Random

23	30	2	8	15	18	6	7	0	21
26	29	17	19	12	3	16	4	24	27
22	28	11	9	13	10	14	5	1	20	25

FIGURE 8.10 Number recognition sheet

left and right sides. For some children, Becky may cover these and only show the center of the sheet.)

Third, Becky asks the child to write any number symbols she knows.

Finally, Becky asks the child to count sets of objects. She begins by asking him to count a random set of between fifteen and twenty-five objects on the table. Then she asks him to create sets of five, ten, and twenty objects by removing them from a bucket.

When Becky interviews a student, she documents the process by filling in the form shown in Figure 8.11. Over the years

---

Kindergarten Number Assessment Interview

Student's Name: _____   Date: _____

ROTE COUNTING:

How high can you count?

Child's prediction (if given): _____

Sequence counted: _____

_____

Can you count any other way?

Backwards: _____   By 10's _____

By 5's: _____   By 2's _____

In another language: _____

_____

NUMBER RECOGNITION: (Show child sheet of random numbers.)

23	30	2	8	15	18	6	7	0	21
26	29	17	19	12	3	16	4	24	27

| 22 | 28 | 11 | 9 | 13 | 10 | 14 | 5 | 1 | 20 | 25 |

Strategy used for identifying numbers:

at random   counting order

left to right across the page   prompts in classroom

other:_____

FIGURE 8.11 Kindergarten number assessment interview

WRITING NUMBERS (Give each child a blank grid.)

    Writes with right or left hand

    Formation of numbers _____

    Notes about numbers chosen to write: _____

    _____

COUNTING OBJECTS:

    A. Place a group of 15-25 objects on the table. Ask student to count the objects. (Watch for one-to-one correspondence, techniques for keeping track, and number sequence used.)

    B. With objects in basket nearby, ask student to create a set of 5, 10, and 20 objects. (Note any strategy used for moving from one group to the next.)

    Makes a new set each time.

    Uses known set and counts on to new number.

    Demonstrates some knowledge of combining/adding groups.

FIGURE 8.11   Kindergarten number assessment interview (*continued*)

she has developed a coding system to help her complete the form as completely as possible in the available time. Look at the notes she made about the first two tasks in Jamal's interview (see Figure 8.12). Under rote counting, Becky recorded several pieces of information about his response to *Can you count any other way?* The circled *1* indicates that without any further prodding, Jamal counted by tens. The circled *T* and *2* indicate that since Jamal did not provide any further information, Becky asked if he could count backward. When Jamal said, "From one hundred?" with great surprise, Becky suggested twenty. The star shows that Jamal did count backward from ten to one successfully. Becky never

FIGURE 8.12 Two tasks in Jamal's assessment interview

provides more than one prompt, however, because she is most interested in what the children provide on their own.

Next, note the circled *SC* in the number recognition section. From these annotations Becky can remember that Jamal first identified *21* as *12*. He dealt with the numbers in linear order, and when he came to the actual *12*, he pointed back to the *21* and corrected himself.

Throughout an interview, Becky tries to listen without making judgments. Her goal is to collect evidence, not to teach. If she is to maintain the child's trust, it is important that nothing about Becky's facial expressions or words suggests failure or that an inappropriate response has been given. Becky wants to be very sure that her students don't become fearful or hesitant to perform in front of her or to explain their thinking. Becky is also convinced that a number of teachers examining the same child implementing the same tasks in the same way will probably draw different conclusions. She knows she pays closest attention to the things she values most. While she tries to broaden her perspective by listening to others who also have a stake in the matter, such as first-grade teachers and parents, she knows that instruction and assessment are subjective. Many of her students will stand out in first grade for their ability to talk about their mathematical thinking. Many may also be noticed for their "poor" writing of numerals. While Becky values good handwriting, she is much more interested in the development of ideas. Fortunately, over time and by encountering a variety of teachers, her students will acquire a wide range of abilities.

The greatest value of this assessment interview comes when it is repeated. Data gathered over time allow Becky readily to identify a student's growth. Compare Lisa's October interview (Figure 8.13) with the interview Becky conducted with Lisa in May (Figure 8.14). The changes are quite striking. In October Lisa consistently skipped eleven, thirteen, or fifteen or repeated fourteen when counting. Noting Lisa's difficulty with the teen numbers, Becky was able to focus on them when Lisa was involved in counting activities. The May interview shows that Lisa can now count to thirty-nine. (Since it is May, Becky is more comfortable asking Lisa specifically about the other ways to count.) Lisa's ability to recognize numerals has also increased. Becky knows that many children confuse symbols for twelve and twenty-one and is not concerned that this remains a problem for Lisa. Lisa also demonstrates much improvement in her ability to write numerals, even though three, six, and nine continue to be problematic. Not only has she written more examples, her lines and curves are those of a more confident and skilled writer.

Kindergarten Number Assessment Interview

Student's Name: _Lisa_____ Date: __10-9-97__

ROTE COUNTING:

How high can you count?

Child's prediction (if given): _"I think I can count to ...sometimes_
I count backwards and forwards cause
Sequence counted: _____it gets so hard."_____

_1-10_ _12, 14, 14, 15-29 20-29 "I counted to 29."_

Can you count any other way?

ⓣ Backwards: _"10-2 blast-off!."_   By 10's _____

By 5's: _____   By 2's _____

In another language: _"I sort of mix up English, German_
"uno, dos, tris, cuatro, cinco, seis" _and Spanish_

NUMBER RECOGNITION: (Show child sheet of random numbers.)

"I'm sort of mixed up with 6+9.
25 28 Is this 9?"

23	30	2 ✓	8 ✓	(15)	(18)	(6)	7 ✓	0 ✓	(21)	12
26	29	17	19	12	3	16	4	24	27	
22	28	11	9	13	10	14	5	1	20	25

Strategy used for identifying numbers:

(at random)   counting order

left to right across the page   prompts in classroom

other:_____

FIGURE 8.13   Lisa's October assessment interview

WRITING NUMBERS (Give each child a blank grid.)

(Writes with right) or left hand

Formation of numbers *from bottom up*

Notes about numbers chosen to write: *random*

note eleven as "one, one"

COUNTING OBJECTS:

A. Place a group of 15-25 objects on the table. Ask student to count the objects. (Watch for one-to-one correspondence, techniques for keeping track, and number sequence used.)

(T) *Can you show me how to count these?*

L. touched each bear and moved it to a new place.
Skipped 13, said, 14,14, skipped 15, said 16, 17, 18.
(There were 17.)

B. With objects in basket nearby, ask student to create a set of 5, 10, and 20 objects. (Note any strategy used for moving from one group to the next.)

Used correct number sequence!

(Makes a new set each time.)

Uses known set and counts on to new number.

Demonstrates some knowledge of combining/adding groups.

FIGURE 8.13   Lisa's October assessment interview (*continued*)

Writing Numbers

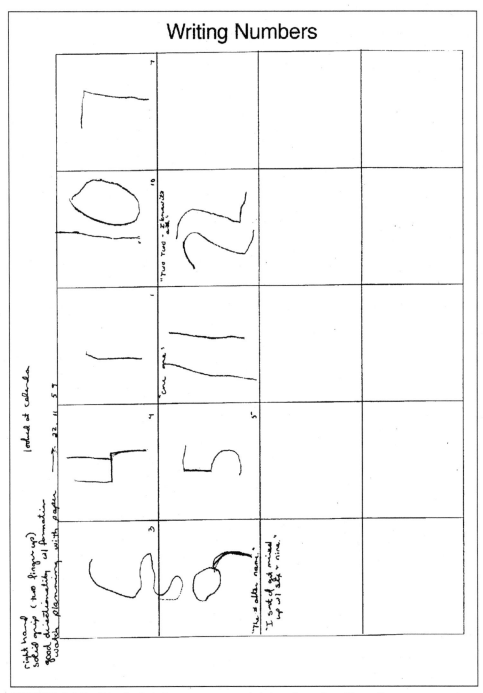

FIGURE 8.13   Lisa's October assessment interview (*continued*)

Kindergarten Number Assessment Interview

Student's Name: _Lisa_   Date: _5·20·98_

ROTE COUNTING:

How high can you count?

Child's prediction (if given): _no response_

Sequence counted: _1-39 "That's all!" Ⓣ what comes next?_

"40" Ⓣ keep going 40-49 Ⓣ keep going "Me don't
know what comes next. 100?"

Can you count any other way?

1 ⓣ Backwards: _11-1_   2 Ⓣ By 10's _10,20 ... 100_

3 ⓣ By 5's: _"no"_   4 Ⓣ By 2's _"no"_

5 ⓣ In another language: _"uno, dos, ... diez"_

NUMBER RECOGNITION: (Show child sheet of random numbers.)

```
  33      ✓      ✓      ✓   ⓢⓒ "55, I mean 15"      ✓      ✓    ✓            12
 ㉓    30     2      8     15✓    18 ✓    6      7     0    ㉑

  "me forget"  ✓      "I already   19         ✓      "me forget"
                    ✓  did this one."
  26     29    17    19   12✓    3✓   ⑯     4    24     27

              ⓢⓒ "6, I mean 9"                      "me forget"
  22✓   28✓   11    9    13✓   10    14✓    5✓    1    20    25
```

Strategy used for identifying numbers:

(at random) 2, 30, 17   counting order

left to right across the page   prompts in classroom

other: _after several random attempts, I pointed↓→ᵣ_
       then she continued this way

FIGURE 8.14 Lisa's May assessment interview

WRITING NUMBERS (Give each child a blank grid.)

    Writes with right or left hand

    Formation of numbers _____

    Notes about numbers chosen to write: _____

COUNTING OBJECTS:

    A. Place a group of 15-25 objects on the table. Ask student to count the objects. (Watch for one-to-one correspondence, techniques for keeping track, and number sequence used.)

Sorted the bears by color after she touched each one.
"21" (correct)

    B. With objects in basket nearby, ask student to create a set of 5, 10, and 20 objects. (Note any strategy used for moving from one group to the next.)

Makes a new set each time.

Uses known set and counts on to new number.

Demonstrates some knowledge of combining/adding groups.

Stopped at 12.
"What number again?"
(T) 20
Continued: 13,14 ... 29
"I got them all mixed up."
Started again at one and counted correctly
to twenty.

FIGURE 8.14 Lisa's May assessment interview (*continued*)

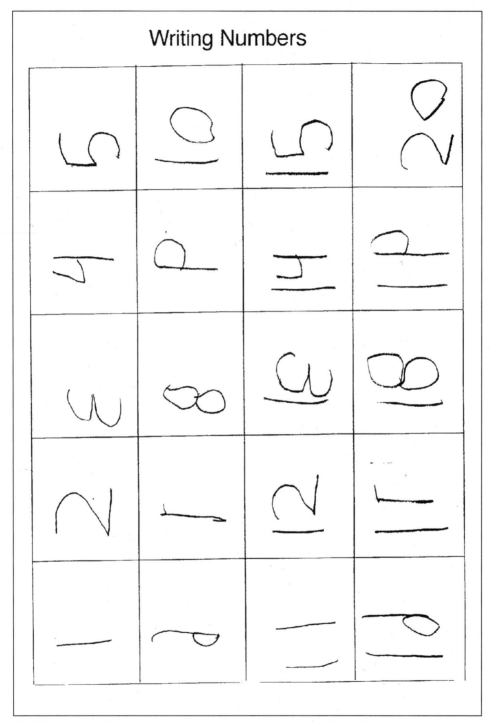

FIGURE 8.14 Lisa's May assessment interview (*continued*)

These interviews take time, and the other children need to work independently during these sessions. It is always helpful to have another resource person in the classroom at such times. Some teachers are fortunate enough to have an assistant or a student teacher, but many do not. There are other sources of extra help, however. Parents and extended family members are obvious ones. Others are college and high school child-development programs; the people who teach and administer them may be eager to identify new field sites. Then, too, middle school and upper elementary school students can assist during specific time periods. Or, Councils on Aging can put you in touch with retired citizens, many of whom may be experienced in working with children or may have other fascinating skills to share with your class. If extra help is not available, Becky conducts interviews while the rest of the children are pursuing explorations. She may interview only one or two children a day or have five or six students do only one of the tasks.

Using Data

The previous chapters of this book include many examples of the ways in which Becky uses what happens in her classroom to help her decide what should happen next. This chapter focuses on the data on which she bases her evaluations of student performance and on how she communicates that performance to others. Student products, anecdotal records, and assessment interview recording sheets help Becky document what her students understand, what skills they have acquired, and what skills remain to be developed. It is through student work, conferences, and report cards that she most often communicates that understanding to other interested parties.

Student Products and Portfolios

One reason Becky emphasizes the representation of mathematical ideas is so that she can collect and examine student products over time. She maintains a file for each child in which she keeps current work and examples of work she wants to save. These files give Becky the powerful ability to demonstrate growth to students and to their parents. It is one thing to tell a child, *I think you write numbers much better now* or *Your representations are much more detailed now.* It is quite another to show children comparative examples and watch their faces beam with pride at their accomplishments. After a given unit of study, Becky sends the work home in a package that includes a description of the work and a comment about the student's progress.

For example, when her students focus on the concept of patterns, Becky makes "pattern pockets" so that she and students can keep track of the patterns they have recorded. When they make patterns with manipulatives, she usually asks them to represent the patterns as drawings on paper, but she will occasionally take a photograph of a particular piece. When Becky reviews this work she looks for the growth of ideas. For example, she notes when children begin to explore patterns other than the basic A–B repeating cycle. At the end of the unit, Becky sends the pattern pockets home with a note. She also includes directions for a game that extends the patterns in the folders. (See Figure 8.15.) The activity allows families to take part in school experiences and gives parents and guardians a clearer sense of what happens in Becky's classroom.

Becky or the student may also select a piece of work to remain in a permanent portfolio. Becky and the child discuss the importance of the work and why it is being saved. At the end of the year, Becky sends the permanent portfolios to the teachers the children will have next year.

Over the years, Becky has adjusted her thinking about student products. She would like to keep everything, but there are daily reminders from wee voices asking, *Can I take this home now?* She has found that if she keeps work too long it may lose meaning for her students. They may simply no longer remember doing the project. She has also learned that if the children participate in the collection and saving process, they remember the activities better. She works hard to find a balance between what, how much, and how long she wants to keep student work and the interests of parents and children, who want it brought home.

Becky has also changed her techniques for "marking" work. When she first began teaching, she relied heavily on worksheets. It was easy to mark a happy face or place a sticker or star on the top of the page. These icons have become trademarks for success,

Dear Families:

Today your child is bringing home his/her pattern pocket. We have all been busy learning about patterns and how they work. The concept of a pattern is very complex and learning about them helps to lay the foundation for understanding other mathematical ideas.

Please take time to have your child show his/her work to you. I know the students are proud of their ideas and are eager to tell you about them. I am attaching directions to a game called, "What Goes Here?" that you can learn to play with your child as another way to focus on the materials they are bringing home.

Have Fun!

☺ Becky

FIGURE 8.15 Becky's pattern pocket cover letter

and everyone knows what they mean. But how can she put just a star on work in a pattern pocket that has been three to four weeks in the making?

At the end of each unit, Becky sits down with each child to review the work going home and to ask a few questions. She includes the children in the assessment of their work; she wants to cultivate habits now that can be fostered as the children get older. Some prompts she finds helpful are:

- How do you feel about your work?
- What is something that was easy for you?
- Tell me something that was hard for you.
- What is something you can tell me about what you have learned?

Some children answer in great detail, while others give one-word responses. If children seem confused or intimidated by these questions, Becky may lead them more directly, interjecting her opinion and then letting the child give his or hers.

Her intention is to help the children feel positive about their learning, not threatened or overwhelmed.

Becky also writes simple but pointed comments on work as opposed to (or in addition to) using a star or a check mark. These brief comments help the parents focus on why the work is important. Examples of comments include:

- Your picture is clear and I can tell how many you counted.
- You asked a lot of people your survey question. I know this took a long time. You were careful to keep track of who you asked.
- You found two different answers to this problem. Do you think there are more?

Sometimes, as in the last example above, she follows the statement with a question so that if parents and children want to, they can extend this work at home. This is not a requirement; home life is busy. But it is a way to open lines of communication with families and to make purposeful responses to the question, *How can I help my child with math at home?*

Conferences and Report Cards
Becky has frequent conversations with parents and guardians throughout the year. She often has the chance to chat with them briefly as they drop off or pick up their children. She invites them to visit the classroom whenever their jobs and other responsibilities allow them to do so. In addition to sending student work home, she prepares informal newsletters that keep families informed about their children's classroom. Through these communications she helps families understand classroom routines, activities, and expectations.

Conferences and report cards build on these informal and more frequent opportunities for communication. In Becky's school system two parent conferences are held (in October and March) and one report card is sent home (in June) each year. Becky enjoys parent conferences. She learns much about her students by interacting with their parents in this sustained period of time.

It is through conferences that parents and guardians learn the most about Becky's mathematical expectations and assessment practices. She explains her record-keeping system to them and shares some of the evidence of their child's performance, thereby letting them know the type of mathematical thinking she values. She never shares all of her documentation at these meetings, of course, because the parents would be overwhelmed. She does, however, support any generalization (*Nicole's number sense has really grown*) with specific examples. Needless to say, families are quite amazed at how much Becky knows about their children.

In Becky's school system report cards are called Progress Reports and the teachers have worked hard to create a form that communicates the curriculum as well as provides data on performance. The section relevant to kindergarten mathematics (see Figure 8.16) indicates a variety of skills and processes. In addition to these descriptions and ratings, there is room for comments. Becky makes at least one comment about each child's math learning. Her data collection and documentation strategies allow her to provide parents with detailed information. Examples include:

> Sarah has moved through our mathematics program in leaps and bounds. It's been very exciting to see her make connections between activities and to tackle increasingly challenging work. Sarah showed a lot of interest in data activities. It was a pleasure to watch her invent her own surveys, collect the data, and then share her findings. She is an excellent problem solver and carefully records her thinking.

> Bobby has solid mathematical skills. He can count with ease to numbers over 100, recites numerous number facts, and takes a vested interest in anything having to do with building. During math workshop Bobby often finishes activities quickly and asks to move on to something else. He provides limited responses when asked to describe and represent his thinking. I would like to see Bobby put more effort into his work and broaden his interests so that he can use his skills more widely.

> As the year ends, Carrie is beginning to show a lot of interest in math workshop. She is more secure with numbers and has worked hard to concentrate when she

Mathematics, Science and Social Studies

Exploration and discovery are at the heart of our kindergarten program. We believe that young children need tangible objects and personal experiences as they discover characteristics about their communities and the world around them. Our goal is to have children become aware of their surroundings, to ask questions, to make observations, and to be respectful of themselves and others. Kindergarten classroom investigations include: seasons/weather, seeds, the five senses, colors, awareness of self and others, nutrition and animals. Throughout the year children are also exposed to the mathematical concepts of patterning, sorting/classifying, geometry, numeration, collecting and recording of data, and the use of non-standard measurement. We introduce numbers as a way to record information and encourage children to use counting as they begin understanding number operations. We look to these elements as the beginning stage of solving problems and we model strategies and skills that proficient problem solvers use.

Understanding of Content

discriminates attributes: size, shape, color

identifies, extends and creates patterns

demonstrates understanding of experiences with data

uses counting accurately as a way to solve problems

compares and orders quantities and numbers

writes numbers to represent quantities

uses manipulatives to show understanding of addition

Reasoning/Process

asks relevant questions

expands vocabulary

answers questions thoughtfully
makes careful observations

predicts outcomes

makes connections

Rating Key for Academic Areas:
NS = needs support on a regular basis in learning
SD = steadily developing independence in learning
IA = independently applies learning

FIGURE 8.16   A kindergarten progress report on mathematics, science, and social studies

is counting and to keep track of her work. This shows significant growth. Please keep her counting over the summer and encourage her to talk about what she knows about numbers, patterns, and shapes. Carrie's mathematics vocabulary has increased notably this year. It is so important that she is willing to speak up and ask when she is unsure of a word.

Becky's use of assessment strategies is a work in progress. It continues to evolve, along with her thinking about teaching and learning. Clearly, she collects an unusual amount of information. She has developed the daily habit of jotting notes to document learning and enjoys doing so. The act of writing helps her pay closer attention to the children's words and actions. She finds that more formal practices help her solidify her data. Over time, collecting this information has helped her understand better the ways in which mathematical ideas develop. By deepening her knowledge of individual children, she has gained a better understanding of all children.

These habits have developed over the years and are now an integral component of her practice. She knows she will continue to revise her recording sheets and to wonder about just how much and exactly what she should document. She has learned to look forward to the next "assessment moment," just as she looks forward to "teachable moments." Often, they are one and the same.

9

A Problem Worth Revisiting

Focusing on big ideas does not mean that practice is not required; it is. Recurring exposure provides children with the repetition they need to develop important concepts and skills. Concepts do not develop quickly. Broad generalizations that support and deepen learning take time to form. By revisiting the same questions throughout the school year, children are encouraged to amplify their mathematical thinking (Mills et al. 1996). They are able to practice, maintain, and build on their new skills and concepts. Through these "revisits," teachers can more easily note developmental patterns among learners and focus their instruction on big ideas.

Several years ago Becky participated in an assessment institute at Lesley College. One of the sessions that particularly piqued her interest was on the characteristics of "good problems." She was confident that she provided her students with "good activities," but she was less sure that she posed "good problems." Was it possible to do so at the kindergarten level?

This chapter was previously published, in a different form, in the October, 1998, issue of *Teaching Children Mathematics*. Used with permission from the National Council of Teachers of Mathematics.

Throughout the following year a few teachers who had taken part in the institute met informally to discuss their efforts at implementing ideas in their classroom. That June, Becky decided to try a problem that had been suggested at one of the group's meetings. It is different from a standard addition problem in that it allows the children to find more than one possible answer:

The Snack

Jackie has raisins and carrots for snack.
He has 7 pieces of food altogether.
How many of each could he have?
How many carrots? How many raisins?

After exploring the problem with her students, Becky was sure the problem met the criteria for a good problem:

- It involved significant mathematics.
- It captured the interest of the children and required them to interpret meaning as a group.
- It allowed for multiple entry points, solutions, and recording techniques.
- It encouraged children to invent their own recording schemes and descriptive terms.
- It was easy to represent with physical materials as well as by drawing.
- It could be adapted to fit a variety of contexts, depending on the curriculum and the children's interest.

She decided to explore the problem again the following year.

Becky now has her students investigate this type of problem several times throughout the second half of the year. With each revisit, the numbers vary and the context changes based on current themes and interests, but the problem structure remains the same.

Beginning the Investigation

This year Becky again introduces the problem midyear. *Just Plain Fancy*, by Patricia Polacco (1990), a story about Naomi and Ruth's one fancy egg, has recently captured the children's interest, so

Becky adopts that context. The children gather at the meeting area and Becky reads the problem displayed on the math easel.

Eggs

Naomi and Ruth have 6 eggs.
Some are plain and some are fancy.
How many of each could they have?
How many are plain? How many are fancy?

She rereads the problem several times, the children chiming in. After the children can retell the problem on their own, a discussion ensues.

BECKY:	HOW SHOULD WE BEGIN?
LUKE:	I think I know. It's three plain and three fancy.
TALI:	I don't think we can know.
SETH:	Yes, we can. It's three and three.
KAITLIN:	It doesn't have to be.
JOSÉ:	I think they might have more fancy.
ANA:	Maybe they are all fancy.
LISA:	Maybe they have six plain and six fancy.
NICOLE:	I don't think they can have that many.
MARIO:	I think they can.
ORIN:	I think we should try it.

Since it is the second half of the school year, the children are familiar with classroom expectations. Becky designates workspaces and hands out recording sheets. Children gather into groups and share manipulatives. Many students choose to use stones, perhaps because of their roundness. Others draw pictures of eggs. There are also some plastic eggs in the classroom, and Becky has made some felt eggs for the children to use on the math easel. Some are plain white, some are white with glitter.

Luke and Seth rely on their earlier thinking and quickly arrive at a solution of three plain and three fancy. Most of the other children use a guess-and-test strategy. They are not trying to find all the possible answers; they are searching for one collection of plain and fancy eggs that meets the problem's conditions. They appear to be enthralled with the question and to receive great satisfaction when they discover a solution. As usual, the children record their work. Lisa's representation (Figure 9.1) is typical. A couple of the children make drawings of the manipulatives they use to solve the problem (Ezra's record, Figure 9.2, is one example). They do not use numbers in these initial representations.

Once they find a solution, the children do not search for alternate answers. Becky tries to elicit other ideas by asking, "Do you think there is another way?" Some children respond posi-

FIGURE 9.1 Lisa's solution to the egg problem

Eggs

Naomi and Ruth have 6 eggs.
Some are plain and some are fancy.
How many of each could they have?
How many plain? How many fancy?

FIGURE 9.2 Ezra draws the cubes he used to find his solution

tively but do not search for possibilities. For the most part, children are satisfied when single solutions are found and move on to other activities. After all the children have completed the task, Becky calls them to a meeting. She distributes their recording sheets, placing them on the rug just in front of the children. The sheets help the children remember their work and are used to record additional ideas over the course of the investigation.

BECKY: WHO WOULD LIKE TO SHOW US WHAT YOU FOUND? [*Almost all the children raise their hand.*] MEI, WHY DON'T YOU START. COME UP AND USE THESE FELT PIECES ON THE EASEL TO SHOW US WHAT YOU FOUND.

MEI: [*Taking her recording sheet with her, looking at her drawing, and then sticking three plain and three fancy felt eggs on the easel*] I have three plain and three fancy. [*She shows her drawing.*]

LUKE: That's what I have.

ALLISON: That's what I found, too!

BECKY: DOES ANYONE ELSE HAVE THIS ANSWER? [*Many hands go up. Becky removes the felt pieces.*] DOES ANYONE HAVE A DIFFERENT ANSWER? BEN.

BEN: [*Coming up to the easel and placing felt pieces*] I have four fancy and two plain, for six.

BECKY: DOES ANYONE ELSE HAVE FOUR FANCY AND TWO PLAIN? [*Four children raise their hand. Becky again removes the felt pieces.*] DOES ANYONE HAVE A DIFFERENT ANSWER? KIMI?

KIMI: [*Coming up to the easel and placing felt pieces*] I have three plain and three fancy.

LUKE: We already did that one.

BECKY: IT'S DIFFICULT TO KEEP TRACK OF ALL THESE ANSWERS, ISN'T IT? I'LL MAKE DRAWINGS TO HELP US REMEMBER.

Becky makes this suggestion in order to model the technique. She wants the children to see a representation that shows more than one answer. She does the drawing, rather than the children, to keep the discussion moving. After showing the two answers given thus far, she again asks for alternative solutions. This time, as Rosita places one plain and five fancy felt eggs on the easel, Becky simultaneously makes a drawing on the chart paper clipped to the math easel.

Sharing their work in this way, the children see clearly that there is more than one answer to the problem. At this point, however, they are more interested in who found the same answers they did than in the realization that multiple answers are possible.

The next day Becky reviews the problem and asks each child to find another answer. Work continues in the same manner as the day before, and the children still appear to be highly engaged. Later, when they share their work, they begin to focus on the different possible answers as well as on who has found solutions that are the same as theirs. They take turns giving answers and placing felt pieces on the easel. Becky draws each solution on the chart paper and asks, "Does anyone else have this answer?" The children work hard at deciding which responses are different and which are the same.

LUKE: I have two plain and four fancy.

BECKY: [*After drawing the solution and asking children with the same answer to identify themselves*] DOES ANYONE HAVE A DIFFERENT ANSWER?

RORY: I have four fancy and two plain.

TREVOR: I don't think that is different.

BECKY: CAN YOU TELL US WHY?

TREVOR: [*Pointing to Luke's recording sheet*] Well, see, here's two plain and four fancy. [*He points to Rory's recording sheet.*] Rory has two plain and four fancy, too.

ALLISON: They're just backwards and that's not different eggs.

LISA: I agree with Allison. It's just backwards.

HALEY: You still have the same eggs even if the others are first. But, see, mine is different. [*She holds up a drawing of one plain and five fancy.*]

BECKY: HOW DO YOU KNOW YOURS IS DIFFERENT?

HALEY: I have one plain egg and Trevor and Rory have two.

SAMMY: Yeah, that's different.

Becky is pleased with the way in which the children are able to distinguish what is different and what is the same. She knows that this distinction needs to be made several times but is delighted that they have already found language for talking about this idea. They are beginning to explore some important notions of combining groups of objects.

Negotiating Meaning

The next week, Becky poses a similar problem:

The Nature Walk

On the nature walk we saw 5 animals.
We saw some birds and some bunnies.
How many of each did we see?
How many birds? How many bunnies?

The children explore the problem independently and again record their findings. Birds and bunnies take time for the children to draw. Many of them make detailed drawings (see Mario's record, shown in Figure 9.3). This time a couple of children find more than one possible answer. Ben draws rings around three different solutions (see Figure 9.4). Allison draws two horizontal lines to separate her answers but also draws a vertical line to separate the groups within each solution (see Figure 9.5). The children's recorded work becomes more important to them as they try to keep track of their thinking and to match their findings with the findings of others.

At their meeting there is some discussion about what is dif-

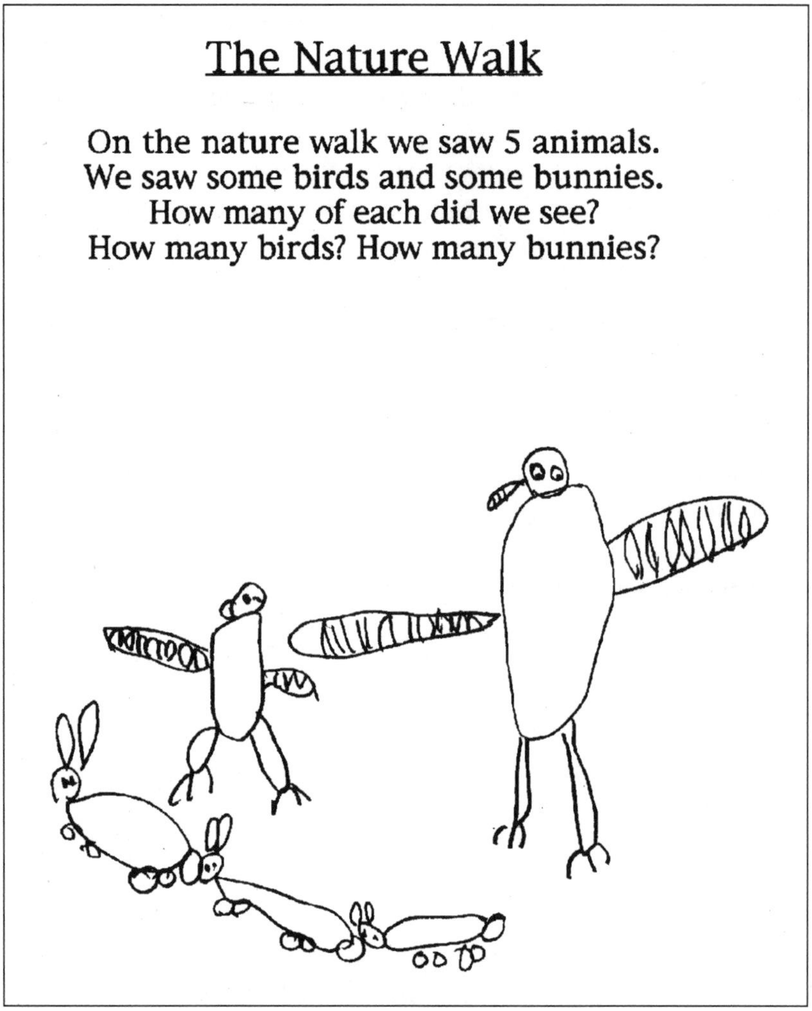

The Nature Walk

On the nature walk we saw 5 animals.
We saw some birds and some bunnies.
How many of each did we see?
How many birds? How many bunnies?

FIGURE 9.3   Mario's solution to the nature walk problem

The Nature Walk

On the nature walk we saw 5 animals.
We saw some birds and some bunnies.
How many of each did we see?
How many birds? How many bunnies?

FIGURE 9.4   Ben draws rings around his solutions

ferent; once again they decide that "backwards" is not different. There is an interesting discussion about whether there must be both bunnies and birds.

TANYA: I got five bunnies and zero birds.

LUKE: There has to be some birds.

TANYA: Why?

LUKE: It asks how many of each. You have to tell how many of each.

The Nature Walk

On the nature walk we saw 5 animals.
We saw some birds and some bunnies.
How many of each did we see?
How many birds? How many bunnies?

FIGURE 9.5 Allison draws lines to separate her answers and the groups within her solutions

ROSITA: Zero tells how many.

HALEY: But there were some birds and some bunnies.

NICOLE: So there should be some.

TANYA: Okay. There has to be some of each.

BECKY: DOES EVERYONE AGREE THAT THERE HAS TO BE SOME BIRDS
AND SOME BUNNIES? [*Everyone nods his or her head, and
Tanya looks pleased.*]

MARIO: So how much is some?

MEGAN: Two is some.

HALEY: Three is some.

TREVOR: It can be any number.

It is important to Becky that the children negotiate problem interpretations for themselves whenever possible. Over the years she has gotten better at stepping back and letting these conversations happen without her interference. She has learned to trust that most of the time the children will eventually straighten things out for themselves. She steps in to help only when they remain confused over a period of time. Zero is an important concept for young children, and Becky is pleased that Tanya is able to draw her own conclusion and thus does not experience a sense of failure for using it in her answer.

The children continue to search for different solutions. The next day Nicole asks Becky, "Can I just draw one bunny and write a three?" Becky asks Nicole to share her idea (see Figure 9.6) during a class meeting. When she does, Trevor responds with excitement, "That's just like two plus three!" With Becky's prodding, the children identify the addition expression for each of the solutions listed thus far.

The next morning Jamal arrives and says, "Can I have a blank bunnies sheet? I thought of a new way to do it." He gets a work can and goes to the art center. In about fifteen minutes he returns with his new representation (see Figure 9.7). He explains his thinking to Becky: "There can be four birds and one bunny, three birds and two bunnies, and two birds and three bunnies. You don't have to draw each one." As Jamal speaks he points his finger to each number on his recording sheet. He continues, "A list is better. I thought of it just as I went to sleep last night." He looks quite proud of his work, and rightfully so.

Emerging Strategies

In April, during a unit on the human body that includes consideration of healthy foods, Becky introduces the original snack problem, with seven carrots and raisins. As is often the case at this age, the children interweave play into their explorations. Kimi arranges her orange rods and small stones to look like a face. Orin and Lisa pretend to eat the carrots and raisins. Playing like

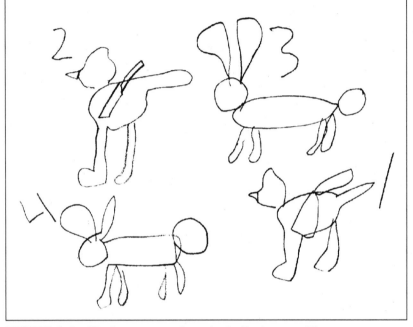

The Nature Walk

On the nature walk we saw 5 animals.
We saw some birds and some bunnies.
How many of each did we see?
How many birds? How many bunnies?

FIGURE 9.6   Nicole uses numbers to indicate quantity

this is a way for the children to relate to the problem and make it their own.

The greater total number of objects challenges many of the students. Rory's representation (see Figure 9.8) shows seven raisins and seven carrots. Ben sees Rory's work and reminds him, "The seven is what you get when you count the raisins and the carrots." The look on Rory's face tells Ben his explanation is not sufficient. Ben then picks up his own drawing (see Figure 9.9) and counts the seven items for Rory. Then he counts Rory's carrots and says, "See. I got to seven and I haven't done the raisins yet." Rory goes off to try again.

The Nature Walk

On the nature walk we saw 5 animals.
We saw some birds and some bunnies.
How many of each did we see?
How many birds? How many bunnies?

FIGURE 9.7   Jamal's solution to the nature walk problem

Kimi uses random trial and error. Working with orange and brown cubes, she takes a handful of each, puts them together, and counts to check. When the total is not seven, she returns the materials to their respective piles and tries again. On her fourth try, she counts seven and is quite pleased with her success. She makes a representation (see Figure 9.10), brings it to Becky, and says, "I got it." When Becky asks her if she can find another way, Kimi meekly shakes her head no.

Luke also uses trial and error, but he adjusts his initial guesses. He takes some felt raisins and some felt carrots and counts to check. He finds that he has six raisins and two carrots. Then he counts the eight felt pieces together. Next, he removes

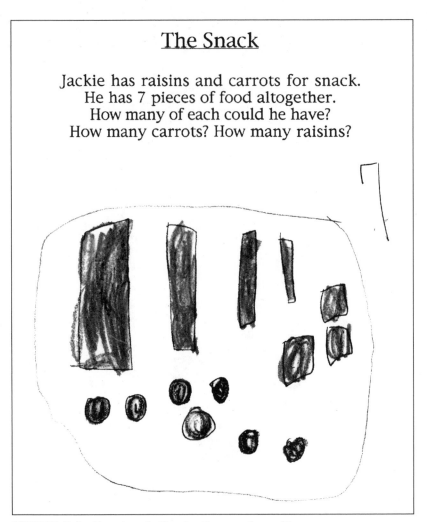

The Snack

Jackie has raisins and carrots for snack.
He has 7 pieces of food altogether.
How many of each could he have?
How many carrots? How many raisins?

FIGURE 9.8   Rory's solution to the snack problem

one of the raisins and recounts. He uses a drawing, numerals, and words to represent his solution. Once this representation is completed, he takes another random collection of carrots and raisins and follows a similar procedure. Luke's work reminds Becky that some children develop sophisticated strategies but still prefer materials very close to the real objects.

Jamal uses orange rods and stones, and at first he is stymied. He moves the materials around and stares at them a while. He is sitting next to Haley, and Becky is nearby.

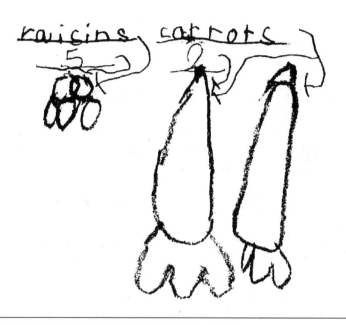

The Snack

Jackie has raisins and carrots for snack.
He has 7 pieces of food altogether.
How many of each could he have?
How many carrots? How many raisins?

FIGURE 9.9   Ben's solution to the snack problem

JAMAL: Miss Eston, Does it have to be even?

BECKY: WHAT DO YOU THINK?

HALEY: No. It can't be.

BECKY: HOW DO YOU KNOW THAT?

HALEY: 'Cause four plus four is eight. So it has to be four plus something else.

JAMAL: That's what I was thinking. It can't be.

Freed from having to find a solution where each addend is the same, Jamal begins work eagerly. He develops a replacement technique. He finds a candidate that meets the problem condition, six

FIGURE 9.10   Kimi's solution to the snack problem

carrots and one raisin. He then replaces one carrot with a raisin to yield another answer.

Nicole uses a counting-on strategy. She takes two brown cubes and says, "One, two." Next, she takes orange cubes, one at a time, while counting on to seven. She does this with three brown cubes and four orange cubes and with five brown cubes and two orange cubes as well. Then she streamlines her recording techniques. Rather than drawing an object and recording the number, she records the number and the first letter of the object's name (see Figure 9.11). She calls this her "letter code."

Megan uses the notion of "opposites" to help her identify multiple solutions. Having found four carrots and three raisins as an answer, she records it as well as three carrots and four raisins. She then searches for a solution that she describes as, "different,

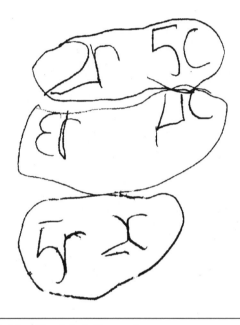

The Snack

Jackie has raisins and carrots for snack.
He has 7 pieces of food altogether.
How many of each could he have?
How many carrots? How many raisins?

FIGURE 9.11   Nicole's letter code

not just opposite." When she finds two carrots and five raisins, she records this answer and its "opposite." (See Figure 9.12.)

While a couple of the children use the term *opposite* when describing their individual work, it has not yet been used in a class discussion. The children have been working on this problem for three days when an important conversation takes place.

BECKY: DO ANY OF YOU THINK YOU HAVE A DIFFERENT ANSWER?
SAMMY: I think we found all of the ways.
TALI: I think so, too. That's all of them.
JOSÉ: I think I see a pattern. There's five and two and two and five. Then three and four and four and three.

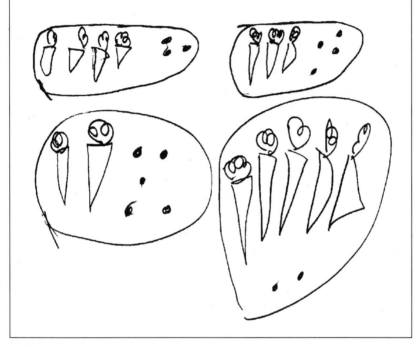

The Snack

Jackie has raisins and carrots for snack.
He has 7 pieces of food altogether.
How many of each could he have?
How many carrots? How many raisins?

FIGURE 9.12   Megan's "opposites"

NICOLE: I see it. There's one and six and six and one.
MEGAN: They're opposites. You get one way and then there is the opposite way.
BECKY: WHAT ARE OPPOSITES?
LUKE: Opposites. You get one and then the other, only opposite.
CHARLIE: These are opposites. [*He points to the 2 + 5 and 5 + 2 shown on the chart paper.*]

The children are excited about this new discovery. Becky wants to make sure they understand the difference between what they are calling an *opposite* and what they earlier called *backwards*. Out of context the commutative property holds: 3 + 4 is equal to 4 + 3. With different labels attached, however, the equivalence relationship no longer exists: 3a + 4b is not equal to 4a + 3b. Becky certainly does not expect the children to formalize these relationships, but she does want them to explore these mathematical ideas informally within this concrete setting.

BECKY: IS FOUR CARROTS AND THREE RAISINS THE OPPOSITE OF THREE RAISINS AND FOUR CARROTS?

ORIN: Yes, four and three is opposite of three and four.

MEGAN: I'm not sure.

ROSITA: Four and three is opposite of three and four.

MEGAN: I don't think so.

BECKY: WHAT COULD WE DO TO FIND OUT?

LISA: We could make it.

JAMAL: We could use rods and stones.

BECKY: [*After asking Jamal to get the materials*] MARIO, WOULD YOU MAKE FOUR CARROTS AND THREE RAISINS? [*Mario counts carefully to make the groups and recounts to check.*] ANA, WOULD YOU MAKE THREE RAISINS AND FOUR CARROTS? [*Ana makes the groups.*] IS THIS SNACK DIFFERENT FROM THIS SNACK?

The children are confused. Most recognize that these snacks are the same, but don't want to let go of their idea of opposites. Becky knows that she needs to help them sort out this complex mathematical idea.

BECKY: WHAT COULD WE DO TO MAKE ONE SNACK DIFFERENT?

BEN: Wait, I have an idea. We can make this one four raisins and three carrots.

BECKY: [*After making the new collection*] IS THIS ONE A DIFFERENT SNACK? [*Several heads nod.*]

MEI: So these two are opposite.

NICOLE: The numbers change, but the carrots have to stay first.

TREVOR: If you have five carrots and two raisins the opposite is two carrots and five raisins.

BECKY: SO WHAT IS THE OPPOSITE OF ONE CARROT AND SIX RAISINS?

SETH: Six carrots and one raisin.

ALLISON: I get it.

Becky knows that some of the children are not clear about this distinction. It is a complicated idea and will need to be revisited several times. What pleases Becky most is that Lisa suggested that they "make it" and Jamal suggested getting materials to portray the examples. It is so important that children learn ways to consider complex ideas from concrete perspectives. Such a strategy will serve them well throughout their mathematical studies.

Children's Recordings

As the children develop recording schemes that require less drawing, they are more likely to arrive at a greater number of possible answers. While we might expect older children to find all combinations, this is not the case in kindergarten. The goal here is to have children explore combining sets as a first step in learning addition. Becky also wants children to investigate problems with more than one answer so that they will develop flexible thinking about numbers and representations.

By the end of the year, a few students will still find only one solution and a few students will find all of the combinations that meet the conditions of the problem. Most students will find several but not all of the possible answers. The recording process becomes particularly important as children begin to find several solutions. It helps children remember the different combinations they have discovered and allows them to bring their thinking to the group.

Most students record their answers by drawing the objects in the problem. A few draw pictures of the manipulatives they used. Usually, the drawing clearly differentiates the two sets within the solution. If more than one answer is found, rings are often drawn around the different solutions. The physical act of drawing or writing, however, provides many challenges at this age. Sometimes it prevents children from finding more answers: the children tire and do not want to draw or write anymore. Sometimes they get so involved in making pictures to represent their findings that the work becomes an artistic endeavor rather than a mathematical representation. With revisits, however, the recording facilitates the children's thinking as they begin to find patterns, create their own picture codes, write words, perhaps even employ conventional symbols.

In late May, a tide pool van comes to Becky's school. The children are fascinated with the hermit crabs and the sea stars. The next day Becky poses the how-many-of-each problem once again, in this context.

In the Tide Pool

There are 8 sea creatures in the tide pool.
Some are hermit crabs and some are sea stars.
How many of each could there be?
How many hermit crabs? How many sea stars?

Since it is late in the year and the fourth time they have explored a version of this problem, their representations are more sophisticated. It may also be that the children are more motivated to find alternative recording schemes because drawing these sea creatures is difficult. When Mei records her first answer, she begins with the three sea stars. Rather than draw the hermit crabs, she draws the cubes she used in her model. She then writes "hermit crabs" to identify what the cubes represent. (See Figure 9.13.)

Rosita uses yellow and blue cubes. She first finds the solution four and four, draws the cubes in her representation, and writes 8. Then she adds a plus sign and an equal sign. She grabs some cubes, adjusts her random guess, and finds an answer of seven sea stars and one hermit crab. She looks at her recording sheet a bit, then says, "I know!" and records a number sentence using numerals and icons. She continues to record her remaining solutions in this manner. (See Figure 9.14.)

Ben works for a long time to find "all of the ways." He also uses cubes and keeps his models on the table as he works. As he finds a new way to show eight, he checks his other models to make sure the new way is different. His recording is unique. He makes a list of numbers of hermit crabs and sea stars and draws a line between the numbers that together form a group of eight. (See Figure 9.15.)

Children's understanding of informal arithmetic far exceeds

In the Tide Pool

There are 8 sea creature in the tide pool.
Some are hermit crabs and some are sea stars.
How many of each could there be?
How many hermit crabs? How many sea stars?

FIGURE 9.13   Mei's solution to the tide pool problem

their ability to use the standard symbols of arithmetic. Becky encourages children to use invented symbols and recording systems. She believes her students will experience few difficulties in making the transition to conventional techniques, since it is merely a matter of learning a new way to record mathematical ideas they have already constructed and understand. By the end of the year, about one third of the children are using numbers in their representations (without Becky's prompts), which often also include invented coding systems. Recording sheets provide important assessment data, allowing teachers, students, and parents to compare results from these investigations over time.

When a child is ready to move to more conventional record-

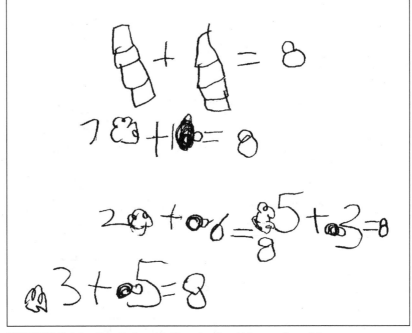

In the Tide Pool

There are 8 sea creature in the tide pool.
Some are hermit crabs and some are sea stars.
How many of each could there be?
How many hermit crabs? How many sea stars?

FIGURE 9.14   Rosita's solution to the tide pool problem

ing techniques, the change can happen quickly. A few years ago Becky's students had planted sunflower seeds and explored seeds that had germinated and seeds that had not. One child made the representation shown in Figure 9.16. When Becky asked him to describe his system, he responded, "The number tells how many. These [pointing to a number in a circle] are the seeds that have not germinated and these [pointing to a number within a double arc] have. There are lots of opposites. When you put them together [tracing the horizontal lines within the symbol between the numbers], you get a total of eight seeds." Becky asked if there was another way to record this. The child's eyes grew wide. "I've

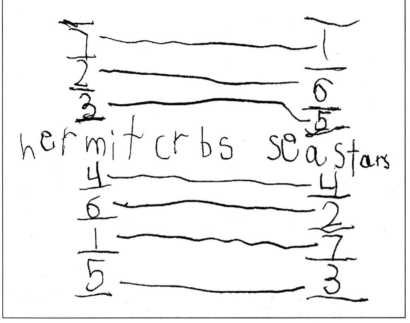

In the Tide Pool

There are 8 sea creature in the tide pool.
Some are hermit crabs and some are sea stars.
How many of each could there be?
How many hermit crabs? How many sea stars?

FIGURE 9.15   Ben's solution to the tide pool problem

got to do this over," he exclaimed. The representation shown in Figure 9.17 was the result. Note his inclusion of zero as an addend and his apparent use of "opposites." Even this child, when asked if he had found all of the ways, responded, "I think so."

Developing Other Contexts

During the past few years, Becky has revisited the how-many-of-each problem within several contexts. One year a child brought in a present to show at the morning meeting, a Colombian basket with five dolls inside. The children were quite intrigued with the way the dolls fit inside the basket and took turns taking them out and placing them back inside the basket. After every-

Sunflower Seeds

We planted 8 sunflower seeds.
Some seeds have germinated and some have not.
What might the cups look like now?

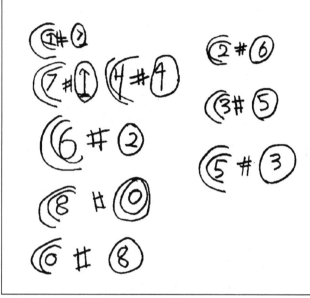

FIGURE 9.16   A child's "double arc" and "circle" shorthand

one had investigated the dolls, Becky said, "Close your eyes so you can't see the basket. How many dolls are inside? How many dolls are outside?"

Another time an amaryllis plant with five buds was given to the class. As the buds turned to blossoms throughout the week the question became, "How many buds and how many blossoms?" One Valentine's Day, the focus was a box with six hearts inside, some red and some white.

There is a bird feeder outside a window in Becky's classroom. Last year the children were unusually interested in the different types of birds that ate at the feeder. This led to a general interest in the identification of birds. Most of the children recognized robins and blue jays. Chickadees and sparrows visited the

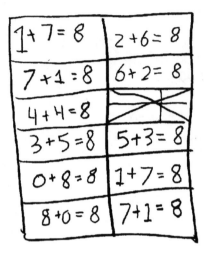

Sunflower Seeds

We planted 8 sunflower seeds.
Some seeds have germinated and some have not.
What might the cups look like now?

$1 + 7 = 8$	$2 + 6 = 8$
$7 + 1 = 8$	$6 + 2 = 8$
$4 + 4 = 8$	
$3 + 5 = 8$	$5 + 3 = 8$
$0 + 8 = 8$	$1 + 7 = 8$
$8 + 0 = 8$	$7 + 1 = 8$

FIGURE 9.17   The child whose solution is shown in Figure 9.16 devises a more traditional representation

feeder frequently and many of the children recognized them as well. One day a male cardinal was flying around outside the window and drew much attention. This led to the problem involving six birds, some sparrows at one bird feeder and some cardinals at another.

Sometimes the context is motivated by literature, as it was this year. *I Am Eyes • Ni Macho* (Ward 1978), an African tale that encourages readers to be aware of their surroundings, motivated exploration of a basket of eight pieces of fruit, some of which were pineapples. When Becky asked the children what else could be in the basket, they chose pears because alliteration plays a prominent role in the story.

These problems are not all at the same level of difficulty. A greater total number of objects makes the investigation more challenging. Children find a solution candidate more easily when the total number of objects is even; many identify the "doubles" answer readily. Whether or not the objects are difficult to draw is also relevant, which is why Becky saves the hermit crabs for the end of the year. The amaryllis problem is simple, because it requires merely that the state of affairs be recorded each day. However, the total also decreases by one each time a blossom falls off. The tangible dolls in the basket are an easy introduction to the problem, while the imagined fruits in the basket are more appropriate for a later revisit.

The types of objects in the collections also have an impact on the ways children think about the problems. Problems with objects that differ only in color, such as white and red hearts in a box, create interesting discussions. Some children view a different arrangement of the red and white cubes used to represent the hearts—for example, two white, two red, and two white rather than four white and two red—as a different solution. Though this could lead to explorations of permutations, such a topic is not mathematically appropriate for most kindergartners.

This type of thinking isn't triggered when the problem places the objects in two different locations or the two groups differ by more than color. Carrots and raisins work well because they differ significantly in color and shape. Bananas and strawberries work equally well. Such groupings allow children to use color to represent their ideas easily but are different enough in other ways not to distract them into thinking a different order matters.

Every year, Becky has her students explore the how-many-of-each problem four or five times. That many repetitions, over time, allow children to deepen their thinking without becoming bored by the tasks or viewing them as routine. Usually, it is the third or fourth revisit before someone connects the problems. When Kaitlin says, "This is like the plain and fancy eggs problem!" broad generalizations are beginning to form in her mathematical thinking.

Regardless of the specific context, the activity unfolds in much the same way each time. Although Becky mediates the context, it is motivated by something that occurs within the classroom. When she has prepared the problem in advance, she presents it to the whole class on the math easel. Children then explore the question individually, within small independent groups, or within a teacher-supported group, depending on their learning needs.

Manipulatives such as rods and cubes are available at all times, as are real objects or felt cutouts representing real objects. When this type of problem is revisited several times during the school year, patterns emerge as to the materials children use to represent the situations. It is clear that different children require different concrete materials to explore these problems successfully. Some children must use very real representations of the items involved, while others can use more generic counters or blocks. The degree to which a manipulative better matches the real item, perhaps in terms of color or shape, is often important. Orange rods and small stones work particularly well for carrots and raisins. Given the different needs of learners, it is important to have several kinds of materials available.

The total number of objects needed to explore the problem also differs. Some children physically represent their first answer and then use new materials to represent each additional answer they find. Once they decide they are through finding solutions, they record their work. Other children use the materials to find an answer, record that answer, and then reuse their materials. When children begin to recognize an answer to the problem immediately (doubles, usually), they often move directly to the recording stage without using materials at all. They then return to materials to find another way to meet the conditions of the problem.

After the children have recorded their work, they bring it to a class meeting. Becky records an answer as it is given, and everyone then discusses whether it is the same or different from the previous answers recorded. The exploration and sharing process continues for two to four math workshops.

Sharing and recording are essential components of these explorations. They help the children define and revise the mathematical concepts embedded in the problem. When children use different materials and recording techniques in the exploration of a question that interests them and find multiple solutions, the likelihood of authentic sharing increases. The children do not just listen to one another politely; they want to hear what others have to say. They are united as a community of learners; the voices of all participants are heard and respected. They negotiate meaning together and create terms to describe their findings.

Some Thoughts in Conclusion

Young children can sustain interest in significant mathematical questions when those questions relate to their personal and classroom experiences and have a variety of entry points. Providing children with opportunities to share and record findings encourages the invention of terms and symbols that have meaning. These inventions lead easily to the conventional forms.

Revisiting a problem throughout the school year provides opportunities for children to build important generalizations. The revisits allow mathematical ideas, strategies, and skills to unfold for both teachers and children. The recording sheets and annotated observations generated by these problems yield important assessment data; changes between revisits are easily noted.

Over the course of several years, only one child in Becky's classroom ended the year by finding all the possible ways for a combination of eight in a systematic sequence and announced proudly that she knew she had found all the ways. For most children, this type of problem may continue to be explored during first and second grade. The growing of mathematical ideas continues as older children describe their thinking as well as record their solutions.

Becky likes to end her mathematical year with a how-many-of-each problem, because it so clearly shows the children's growth. These final weeks are always an emotional time. She feels good about everything her students have shared and accomplished. She knows they will continue to be curious about mathematics and are more confident as learners. She is tired and looking forward to summer and the renewal its different focus inspires. Yet it is so hard to imagine leaving these children with whom she has lived so closely in her classroom.

The children also find it difficult to leave, even though they, too, look forward to the summer. During the end of May, Allison and Tanya are trying to figure out how many days of school remain.

Becky notices them using a pointer and diligently counting the bottom two rows on the number-of-days-in-school chart. The girls come bounding over to her.

ALLISON: Miss Eston, do you know how many days we have left in school?

BECKY: I'M NOT POSITIVE. HOW COULD YOU FIND OUT?

TANYA: We are trying to do that.

ALLISON: We are trying to see how many days are left. I think it's seventeen.

TANYA: I think it's eighteen.

BECKY: HOW DID YOU FIGURE THIS OUT?

ALLISON: I counted all of the blank squares.

TANYA: I did, too. But I also think you need to count today. That makes it one more.

BECKY: HMM, THAT'S TRICKY. ALLISON, WHAT DO YOU THINK ABOUT THIS?

ALLISON: I don't think you need it, because today is today.

TANYA: Yeah, but it's not over yet, so you do need it. It makes eighteen.

ALLISON: No, seventeen! Miss Eston, what do you think?

BECKY: WELL, I THINK YOU ARE BOTH RIGHT. IF YOU COUNT TODAY, IT IS EIGHTEEN. IF YOU DON'T, IT'S SEVENTEEN. WHAT SHOULD WE DO?

ALLISON: Maybe it should be eighteen. I don't want school to end.

TANYA: Me either.

BECKY: I KNOW. WHAT AM I GOING TO DO WITHOUT ALL OF YOU?

ALLISON: I guess you're going to have to get new kids!

BECKY: YES, I GUESS I WILL.

And so it continues.

Appendix A

References for Using Children's Literature

Burns, Marilyn. *Math and Literature (K–3), Book One*. Sausalito, CA: Math Solutions, 1992.

Griffiths, Rachel, and Margaret Clyne. *Books You Can Count On*. Portsmouth, NH: Heinemann, 1991.

Schiro, Michael. *Integrating Children's Literature and Mathematics: Children as Meaning Makers, Problem Solvers, and Literary Critics*. New York: Teachers College Press, 1997.

Sheffield, Stephanie. *Math and Literature (K–3), Book Two*. Sausalito, CA: Math Solutions, 1995.

Thiessen, Diane, and Margaret Matthias. *The Wonderful World of Mathematics*. 2d ed. Reston, VA: National Council of Teachers of Mathematics, 1998.

Welchman-Tischler, Rosamond. *How to Use Children's Literature to Teach Mathematics*. Reston, VA: National Council of Teachers of Mathematics, 1992.

Whitin, David, and Sandra Wilde. *It's the Story That Counts: More Children's Books for Mathematical Learning, K–6.* Portsmouth, NH: Heinemann, 1995.

———. *Read Any Good Math Lately? Children's Books for Mathematical Learning, K–6.* Portsmouth, NH: Heinemann, 1992.

Appendix B

*Twenty-Five Favorite Books for Supporting Mathematics
Instruction in the Kindergarten Classroom*

Accorsi, William. *Billy's Button.* New York: Greenwillow, 1992.

Aker, Suzanne. *What Comes in 2's, 3's, & 4's?* New York: Simon &
Schuster, 1990.

Anno, Mitsumasa. *Anno's Counting Book.* New York: Crowell,
1977.

Bang, Molly. *Ten, Nine, Eight.* New York: Greenwillow, 1983.

Barker, Celia. *One Watermelon Seed.* Toronto: Oxford University
Press, 1985.

Carle, Eric. *The Secret Birthday Message.* Hong Kong:
HarperCollins, 1972.

———. *The Very Hungry Caterpillar.* New York: Putnam, 1989.

Crews, Donald. *Ten Black Dots.* New York: Greenwillow, 1986.

Dale, Penny. *Ten in the Bed.* Pleasant Hill, CA: Discovery Toys,
1988.

———. *Ten Out of Bed.* Cambridge, MA: Candlewick, 1993.

Freeman, Don. *A Pocket for Corduroy.* New York: Viking, 1978.

Hamm, Diane Johnston. *How Many Feet in the Bed?* Books for Young Readers. New York: Simon & Schuster, 1991.

Hellen, Nancy. *The Bus Stop.* New York. Orchard, 1988.

Hoban, Tana. *All About Where.* New York: Greenwillow, 1991.

———. *Push–Pull, Empty–Full.* New York: MacMillan, 1972.

———. *Shapes, Shapes, Shapes.* New York: Greenwillow, 1986.

Hopper, Meredith. *Seven Eggs.* Hong Kong: HarperCollins, 1985.

Liebler, John. *Frog Counts to Ten.* Brookfield, CT: Millbrook, 1994.

Lindbergh, Reeve. *The Midnight Farm.* Books for Young Readers. New York: Dial, 1987.

Lobel, Arnold. *Frog and Toad Are Friends.* New York: Harper & Row, 1970.

McMillan, Bruce. *Counting Wildflowers.* New York: Mulberry Paperback, 1986.

Morozumi, Atsuko. *One Gorilla.* New York: Farrar, Strauss & Giroux, 1990.

Onyefulu, Ifeoma. *Emeka's Gift: An African Counting Story.* New York: Cobblehill/Dutton, 1995.

Reid, Margarette. *The Button Box.* New York: Dutton Children's, 1990.

Russo, Marisabina. *The Line-Up Book.* New York: Puffin, 1992.

Bibliography

Accorsi, William. 1992. *Billy's Button*. New York: Greenwillow.

Aker, Suzanne. 1990. *What Comes in 2's, 3's, & 4's?* New York: Simon & Schuster.

Anno, Mitsumasa. 1977. *Anno's Counting Book*. New York: Crowell.

Atkinson, Sue. 1992. "A New Approach to Maths." In *Mathematics With Reason*, edited by Sue Atkinson. Portsmouth, NH: Heinemann.

Bang, Molly. 1983. *Ten, Nine, Eight*. New York: Greenwillow.

Baratta-Lorton, Mary. 1976. *Mathematics Their Way*. Menlo Park, CA: Addison-Wesley.

Barker, Celia. 1985. *One Watermelon Seed*. Toronto: Oxford University Press.

Brooks, Jacqueline, and Martin Brooks. 1993. *The Case for Constructivist Classrooms*. Alexandria, VA: Association for Supervision and Curriculum Development.

Bullock, James. 1994. "Literacy in the Language of Mathematics." *The American Mathematical Monthly* 101(October):735–43.

Burns, Marilyn. 1992. *Math and Literature (K–3) Book One.* Sausalito, CA: Math Solutions.

Carle, Eric. 1972. *The Secret Birthday Message.* Hong Kong: HarperCollins.

———. 1989. The Very Hungry Caterpillar. New York: Putnam.

Carpenter, Thomas, Ellen Ansell, Megan Franke, Elizabeth Fennema, and Linda Weisbeck. 1993. "A Study of Kindergarten Children's Problem-Solving Process." *Journal for Research in Mathematics Education* 24 (November):428–41.

Clements, Douglas. 1996. "Rethinking Concrete Manipulatives." *Teaching Children Mathematics* 2(January):270–79.

———. 1997. "(Mis?)Constructing Constructivism." *Teaching Children Mathematics* 4(December):198–200.

Corwin, Rebecca. 1996. *Talking Mathematics: Supporting Children's Voices.* Portsmouth, NH: Heinemann.

Crews, Donald. 1986. *Ten Black Dots.* New York: Greenwillow.

Dale, Penny. 1988. *Ten in the Bed.* Pleasant Hill, CA: Discovery Toys.

———. 1993. *Ten Out of Bed.* Cambridge, MA: Candlewick.

Davis, Robert. 1992. "Understanding 'Understanding.'" *Journal of Mathematical Behavior* 11(September):225–42.

Economopolous, Karen, and Megan Murray. 1998. *Mathematical Thinking in Kindergarten.* Investigations in Number, Data and Space. White Plains, NY: Dale Seymour.

Economopolous, Karen, Megan Murray, Kim O'Neil, Douglas Clements, Julie Sarama, and Susan Jo Russell. 1998. *Making Shapes and Building Blocks.* Investigations in Number, Data and Space. White Plains, NY: Dale Seymour.

Economopolous, Karen, and Susan Jo Russell. 1998. *Counting Ourselves and Others.* Investigations in Number, Data and Space. White Plains, NY: Dale Seymour.

Eston, Rebeka, and Karen Economopolous. 1998. *Pattern Trains and Hopscotch Paths.* Investigations in Number, Data and Space. White Plains, NY: Dale Seymour.

Feinberg, Sylvia, and Mary Mindess. 1994. *Eliciting Children's Full Potential: Designing and Evaluating Developmentally Based Programs for Young Children.* Pacific Grove, CA: Brooks/Cole.

Fisher, Bobbi. 1991. *Joyful Learning: A Whole Language Kindergarten.* Portsmouth, NH: Heinemann.

Freeman, Don. 1978. *A Pocket for Corduroy.* New York: Viking.

Fromberg, Doris. 1987. *The Full-Day Kindergarten.* New York: Teachers College Press.

Garrison, Leslie. 1997. "Making the NCTM's Standards Work for Emergent English Speakers." *Teaching Children Mathematics* 4(November):132–38.

Gawned, Sue. 1993. "An Emerging Model of the Language of Mathematics." In *Language in Mathematics*, edited by Jennie Bickmore-Brand. Portsmouth, NH: Heinemann.

Ginsberg, Herbert. 1989. *Children's Arithmetic: How They Learn It and How You Teach It.* Austin, TX: ProEd.

Ginsberg, Herbert, and Joyce Baron. 1993. "Cognition: Young Children's Construction in Mathematics." In *Research Ideas for the Classroom: Early Childhood Mathematics*, edited by Robert Jensen. Reston, VA: National Council of Teachers of Mathematics.

Greenes, Carole, and Linda Schulman. 1996. "Communication Processes in Mathematical Explorations and Investigations." In *Communication in Mathematics, K–12 and Beyond*, edited by Portia Elliott. Reston, VA: National Council of Teachers of Mathematics.

Griffiths, Rachel, and Margaret Clyne. 1991. *Books You Can Count On.* Portsmouth, NH: Heinemann.

Hamm, Diane Johnston. 1991. *How Many Feet in the Bed?* Books for Young Readers. New York: Simon & Schuster.

Hellen, Nancy. 1988. *The Bus Stop.* New York: Orchard.

Hiebert, James, et al. 1997. *Making Sense: Teaching and Learning Mathematics With Understanding.* Portsmouth, NH: Heinemann.

Hoban, Tana. 1972. *Push–Pull, Empty–Full.* New York: MacMillan.

————. 1986. *Shapes, Shapes, Shapes.* New York: Greenwillow.

————. 1987. *26 Letters and 99 Cents.* New York: Greenwillow.

————. 1991. *All About Where.* New York: Greenwillow.

Hopper, Meredith. 1985. *Seven Eggs.* Hong Kong: HarperCollins.

Hughes, Martin. 1986. *Children and Number: Difficulties in Learning Mathematics.* Oxford, UK: Basil Blackwell.

Jalango, Mary. 1995 "Promoting Active Listening in the Classroom. *Childhood Education* 72(fall):13–18.

Kamii, Constance. 1985. *Young Children Reinvent Arithmetic: Implications of Piaget's Theory.* New York: Teachers College Press.

Kliman, Marlene, Christopher Mainhart, Megan Murray, and Karen Economopoulos. 1998. *How Many in All? Investigations in Number, Data and Space.* White Plains, NY: Dale Seymour.

Lapan, Glenda. 1993. "What Do We Have and Where Do We Go from Here?" *Arithmetic Teacher* 40(May):524–26.

Lesh, Richard. 1979. "Mathematical Learning Disabilities: Considerations for Identification, Diagnosis and Remediation." In *Applied Mathematical Problem Solving,* edited by Richard Lesh et al. Columbus, OH: ERIC/SMEAC.

Liebler, John. 1994. *Frog Counts to Ten.* Brookfield, CT: Millbrook.

Lindbergh, Reeve. 1987. *The Midnight Farm.* Books for Young Readers. New York: Dial.

Lobel, Arnold. 1970. *Frog and Toad Are Friends*. New York: Harper & Row.

McMillan, Bruce. 1986. *Counting Wildflowers*. New York: Mulberry Paperback Press.

Meira, Luciano. 1995. "The Microevolution of Mathematical Representations in Children's Activity." *Cognition and Instruction* 13(2):269–313.

Mills, Heidi, Timothy O'Keefe, and David Whitin. 1996. *Mathematics in the Making*. Portsmouth, NH: Heinemann.

Moon, Jean, and Linda Schulman. 1995. *Finding the Connections: Linking Assessment, Instruction, and Curriculum in Elementary Mathematics*. Portsmouth, NH: Heinemann.

Morozumi, Atsuko. 1990. *One Gorilla*. New York: Farrar, Straus & Giroux.

Morris, Ann. 1989. *Bread Bread Bread*. New York: Lothrop, Lee & Shepard.

Murray, Megan, Karen Economopoulos, and Marlene Kliman. 1998. *Collecting, Counting and Measuring*. Investigations in Number, Data and Space. White Plains, NY: Dale Seymour.

Nelson, Doyal, and Joan Worth. 1983. *How to Choose and Create Good Problems for Primary Children*. Reston, VA: National Council of Teachers of Mathematics.

National Council of Teachers of Mathematics (NCTM). 1989. *Curriculum and Evaluation Standards for School Mathematics*. Reston, VA: NCTM.

———. 1991. *Professional Standards for Teaching Mathematics*. Reston, VA: NCTM.

———. 1994. *Assessment Standards for School Mathematics*. Reston, VA: NCTM.

———. 1998. *Principles and Standards for School Mathematics: Discussion Draft*. Reston, VA: NCTM.

Olivares, Rafael. 1996. "Communication in Mathematics for Students with Limited English Proficiency." In *Communication in Mathematics, K–12 and Beyond*, edited by Portia Elliott. Reston, VA: National Council of Teachers of Mathematics.

Onyefulu, Ifeoma. 1995. *Emeka's Gift: An African Counting Story.* New York: Cobblehill/Dutton.

Polacco, Patricia. 1990. *Just Plain Fancy.* New York: Bantam Little Rooster.

Reid, Margarette. 1990. *The Button Box.* New York: Dutton Children's.

Reys, Barbara, and Vena Long. 1995. "Teacher as Architect of Mathematical Tasks" *Teaching Children Mathematics* 1(January):296–99.

Richardson, Kathy. 1997. Early Childhood Corner, "Too Easy for Kindergarten and Just Right for First Grade." *Teaching Children Mathematics* 3(April):432–37.

Rowe, Mary. 1986. "Wait Times: Slowing Down May Be a Way of Speeding Up!" *Journal of Teacher Education* 37(January–February):43–50.

Russo, Marisabina. 1992. *The Line Up Book.* New York: Puffin.

Schiro, Michael. 1997. *Integrating Children's Literature and Mathematics: Children as Meaning Makers, Problem Solvers, and Literary Critics.* New York: Teachers College Press.

Schulman, Linda, and Rebeka Eston. 1998. "A Problem Worth Revisiting." *Teaching Children Mathematics* 5(October): 72–77.

Schwartz, Sydney, and Anna Beth Brown. 1995. "Communicating With Young Children in Mathematics: A Unique Challenge." *Teaching Children Mathematics* 1 (February):350–53.

Sheffield, Stephanie. 1995. *Math and Literature (K–3) Book Two.* Sausalito, CA: Math Solutions.

Thiessen, Diane, and Margaret Matthias. 1998. *The Wonderful World of Mathematics.* 2d ed. Reston, VA: National Council of Teachers of Mathematics.

Ususkin, Zalman. "Mathematics as a Language." 1996. In *Communication in Mathematics, K–12 and Beyond*, edited by Portia Elliott. Reston, VA: National Council of Teachers of Mathematics.

Vygotsky, Lev. 1978. *Mind in Society.* Cambridge, MA: Harvard University Press.

Ward, Leila. 1978. *I Am Eyes • Ni Macho.* New York: Scholastic.

Welchman-Tischler, Rosamond. 1992. *How to Use Children's Literature to Teach Mathematics.* Reston, VA: National Council of Teachers of Mathematics.

Whitin, David, and Wilde, Sandra. 1992. *Read Any Good Math Lately? Children's Books for Mathematical Learning, K–6.* Portsmouth, NH: Heinemann.

———. 1995. *It's the Story That Counts: More Children's Books for Mathematical Learning, K–6.* Portsmouth, NH: Heinemann.

Whitin, David, Heidi Mills, and Timothy O'Keefe. 1990. *Living and Learning Mathematics.* Portsmouth, NH: Heinemann.

Wilde, Sandra, ed. 1996. *Notes From a Kidwatcher: Selected Writings of Yetta M. Goodman.* Portsmouth, NH: Heinemann.